The Home Birth Advantage

by Mayer Eisenstein, M. D.

The Home Birth Advantage
Mayer Eisenstein, M. D.

Published by CMI Press
http://www.homefirst.com

ISBN 0-9670444-0-5 $16.95

Text copyright © 2000 Mayer Eisenstein

Printed in the United States of America

Type set in ITC Bookman and ITC Leawood

Dedication

*I*t is with deep personal and professional sadness that I write this posthumous dedication to Dr. Herbert Ratner, who was my mentor, friend, and one of the brightest men in medicine today. Dr. Herbert Ratner passed away in November of 1997. He was very excited and supportive about the message of *The Home Birth Advantage.*

The philosophy of Homefirst® Health Services, my medical practice, is actually Dr. Ratner's philosophy. He was a true scholar and progressive medical doctor who foresaw the future of medicine in America. I like to think of Dr. Ratner as someone who stood for the Hippocratic Oath, someone who believed in primum non nocere, "doing no harm" in his medical practice, someone with a strong belief in the "wait and see" approach to birth.

This birthing system we follow in my practice is one Dr. Ratner taught and encouraged me to implement. The fact that it has become the safest way of having babies in America makes us proud. We have been able to implement so much of his teaching in a system that works best for all healthy pregnant women in America.

Our inspirational mentor will be with us as we watch our system become the most prevalent birthing system in America.

What better tribute than this could I, the disciple, pay to the master?

Acknowledgments

I want to thank my wife, Karen, for 30 years of inspiration and support. She has given me the greatest gifts in life: Jeremy, Jennifer, Alycia, Shoshana, Jordana and Zachary. And now some of my children and their spouses have given me the most wonderful gifts of grandchildren: Jeremy and Susan are the parents of Kayla and Danielle; Jennifer and Dan have given birth to Abigail, Ethan and Jacob. All my grandchildren have been born at home with the support of family around them, all have been breastfed by their wonderful mothers.

Without Karen at my side I would not have become the person, the doctor, the attorney, the father and grandfather I am today. *The Home Birth Advantage* has certainly been inspired by my wife, Karen, and our own home team.

It is with much gratitude that I acknowledge the efforts, personal and professional, which made *The Home Birth Advantage* a reality.

Contents

Contents

 *Author's Note*

The dialogues and monologues quoted in the chapters of this book, unless otherwise stated, are excerpted from the phone-in portion of The Homefirst Family Health Forum, Dr. Eisenstein's nationally syndicated radio program.

Hosting the weekly show has prompted me to collect my thoughts and years of printed material for publication in this book.

I'd like to thank those families who were a part of the call-in portion of The Homefirst Family Health Forum and the many families who allowed themselves to be interviewed in person about their birth and nursing experiences. Many of them are quoted in this book because there is no more powerful way of explaining home birth than through the words of those who have experienced it firsthand. In some cases their names have been changed to preserve anonymity.

Thank you all for sharing these very special moments in your family lives.

Section One

Homefirst
Health Services

Why Me?

"We arrive at truth not by reason only,
but also by the heart."
— Blaise Pascal, Pensées

"*W*hy me?" I've often thought. How did I come to carry the home birth torch? I have always felt so fortunate, so blessed, to have studied under the greatest "birthing gurus" of this century. And I have always wondered why none of my medical school classmates took advantage of the same learning opportunities I had. Why weren't there lines of students at the doors of these wise and wonderful teachers?

After many years of wondering, I think I finally came upon the answer. But, of course, to get to the answer you must bear with me through one of my favorite pastimes - digressing.

But it is digressing with a purpose. I'd like to tell you, "Why me?" and I'd like to tell you, "Why home birth?" and I'd like to tell you, "Why another book on home birth?"

Let me assure you this book is different. I know of no other home birth book which takes the hard core stand that home birth is safer. They say that it is nice. It is more comfortable. It is a friendly alternative to hospital birth. But no one says that it is safer, many times safer than hospital birth.

It is.

And I'd like to tell you why.

So . . . Why me?

Lessons of Life and Medical School

I was not blinded by an inspirational light one day. My decisions to be a doctor, to become involved in infant and maternal care, and to deliver babies at home evolved from the many personal experiences I had as a medical school student and a student of life. I'd like to share some of my story with you because in reading my story you will perhaps come to understand, as I did, that home birth is the only way American women should be giving birth today.

How far back should I go to begin?

For now, I will start with my two boyfriends from grade school. They were both destined from birth to be doctors. I was a good student but they pushed me to be a very good student. They felt I should do as well as they did and keep up my grades because, of course, I should go to medical school also.

These two friends continued their inspirational pushing through grade and high school and into college.

When I graduated with an undergraduate degree in statistics, they were still telling me I belonged in medical school with them. I fancied a master's degree in statistics but didn't really know what I wanted, so off I went to medical school.

The first two years weren't too bad, a lot of reading and memorizing. But by the end of the second year I was losing interest. Then came our first chance to get a peek at what doctoring was all about, a course called "Physical Diagnosis."

The doctors did a very poor job of teaching the course, and I learned nothing about physical diagnosis. We would go around with the doctors and listen to things like heart murmurs. I never could hear them. All the other students said they did, so on we would move to the next patient. I'd be lagging behind saying, "Couldn't we just spend another minute? I don't hear anything."

After class the other students would admit to me that they also heard nothing but were pretending their way through the course. "Wait a minute!" I said. "This isn't grade school. We are becoming doctors and we'll be dealing with people's lives!" Their advice to me was just to pretend I heard everything I was supposed to hear.

I failed the course.

Due to my "failure" I was privileged to really learn physical diagnosis from another significant person in my life, Dr. Ann Peterson, Dean of Students at the University of Illinois Medical School. My "punishment" for failing the course was to go around with Dr. Peterson every Friday to learn physical diagnosis. She was a great teacher. We would spend one whole day learning about the eye, then the heart, lungs, ears. At the end of the summer I was tested and received an "A" in the course. I am a very competent diagnostician today, thanks to Dr. Peterson!

That was a great summer for my career development. My faith in the profession had been restored a bit by this experience. And soon I was to meet the first of my classroom teachers who was a person as well as a physician, Dr. Robert Mendelsohn. I was enrolled in his pediatrics course. He was a phenomenal teacher and the only doctor who had a first name in all of medical school. On the first day of class he introduced himself as Bob Mendelsohn. Unheard of!

Dr. Mendelsohn presented three lectures a week and would take his students on rounds. We felt free to ask all the questions we wanted, and he saw to it that we didn't move on until everyone knew the material. On Fridays he would take anyone to lunch who wanted to go. The agenda was always the same - noon lunch, one o'clock clinic and two o'clock discussion.

I was learning for the first time, in a medical school class, and I couldn't get enough. Dr. Mendelsohn had a way of making you feel so good about what it was you had to contribute to a discussion. There wasn't any subject I could bring up in the medical field in which he wasn't well-versed. He would send his students away fired up to read and learn all they could.

On weekends Dr. Mendelsohn liked to walk over to the public tennis courts near his house and play. Fortunately for me, when I would join him, the courts would be crowded and we would sit and talk pediatrics for hours while waiting for a court. I have to say that my tennis game didn't improve but I surely learned a lot about medicine.

By the time I could decide how I would spend two elective quarters of medical school I received approval to study with Dr. Mendelsohn. I was fortunate enough to spend six months with him doing whatever it was he was doing at the time. I went to his lectures and on rounds at Michael Reese Hospital and helped supervise his staff who gave Head Start exams to preschoolers. At the time he was serving as the Director of Head Start for Cook County. Whatever he was doing, he did it well and with much integrity. It was no wonder that he was one of the nation's leading pediatricians.

Our Own Birth Experience

When my wife, Karen, become pregnant with our first child, I was still in medical school. I called Dr. Mendelsohn for his recommendation of a doctor for us. Karen's obstetrician, who had delivered her, had already told her that natural childbirth was absurd, and she should abandon all thoughts of it. So we went to a recommended doctor who was supposed to be a big proponent of natural childbirth.

However, when Karen actually went into labor, all hopes of natural childbirth went out the window under the care of this man. The labor and delivery of our son was hideous. Karen was sent to bed, flat on her back at the hospital, just as any other doctor would have recommended; and an IV was inserted in her arm. There was nothing natural about it.

I pulled out the IV at her insistence; and after fifteen miserable hours of labor at the hospital, our son Jeremy was born. The doctor barely made it to the room as Karen pushed the baby out. Our new little boy was quickly whisked away from us and put under what Karen called "French fry lights in a little aquarium." We left there as soon as we could, a few hours later. Karen told me that we'd have to find another way to have our children. This had not been an experience she wished to repeat.

At this time I never would have thought of going into obstetrics. My obstetrics rotation in med school had been interesting, but I didn't want to go into that field. No one liked what they were doing in that department. There were all those screaming women, forceps, episiotomies, blood all over the place - as unenjoyable as could be!

The Discovery of Something Magnificent

Dr. Mendelsohn set himself the task of finding a doctor for us so that Karen could foresee having more than one child. When Jeremy was only about ten days old, Dr. Mendelsohn sent me to visit Dr. Gregory White. Dr. White had been quietly doing home births in Chicago's suburbs for many years.

I couldn't get over it!

I attended a birth with him where the labor was almost identical to Karen's — but it was wonderful! The woman was up and walking around till it was time for the actual birth. She had her husband and family around her. There was no episiotomy, forceps or drugs. The birth was a joyful, spiritual experience for the mother, rather than the climax of many fearful and helpless hours spent on her back at the mercy of the medical staff. I was so excited by this experience that I went with Dr. White to another birth and another and another. All were wonderful.

I said to him, "Dr. White, either you have a group of the weirdest women patients I've ever met or you've discovered something magnificent!"

He responded, "Home birth is like this all the time."

After this whenever I could find some spare time, I would spend it with Dr. White. I was in love with what he was doing and each birth was as wonderful as the last. There was nothing like the high that everyone at these home births was feeling. The new mothers were energized and joyful, not sleepy and depressed.

Upon completion of medical school, I was fortunate to be able to work with both Doctors Mendelsohn and White in their practices. Dr. White and I would go on deliveries together. From him I also learned my bedside manner. He was the most patient person in the world and could make everyone feel comfortable. The simplicity of his techniques amazed me. He would watch and watch and watch at a birth, just really watch what was happening and soon the baby would come out.

In between evaluations of the mother's progress, we would sit at the family's kitchen table and discuss obstetrics cases. "A university should consist of a log with a student on one end and a professor on the other," Mark Twain once said. I had certainly found my university!

County Hospital

Soon after Dr. White delivered my second child, Jennifer, at home, he invited me to join him in his practice. So I began working at Cook County Hospital to gain all the obstetrics experience I could before joining him.

I loved County. There were 3,000 babies being born there each month. I could deliver in six months at County more babies than in a four-year university obstetrics program. It was a great learning opportunity.

There was a respect for students at County that I had never felt and a very nice feeling that everyone was helping everyone else through. The senior residents were Pakistanis with a lovely spirit, willing to teach me all they knew about home birth - still prevalent in their country. They didn't understand why I would want to practice this ancient method of childbirth, but if I did they would help me. They called me for all the difficult cases to insure that I would see all types of birth before going into practice.

Meanwhile Dr. White had instructed me to learn all I could at County about forceps deliveries, episiotomies and other intervention techniques because, he said, "You won't learn about these things at home births; they just aren't necessary."

I did learn those techniques, following County's outstanding motto, "See one. Do one. Teach one." But after a while I decided instead to implement at the hospital some of the home birth techniques I had learned. There were certainly plenty of opportunities for implementation. There was a row of fifteen labor rooms at County. The doctors' names would be called over the address system to go to the room where they were needed. "Eisenstein, Room 5."

At first I would drop the episiotomy scissors on the floor and "accidentally" step on them so that they could not be used. Soon I noticed that when I was called from delivery room to delivery room there would never be any episiotomy scissors on my tray. The nurses finally admitted to me, "Who do you think you are fooling! We know you don't do episiotomies, so why should we give you scissors to drop on the floor?"

I became "the specialist" called for every case where the woman didn't want drugs or an episiotomy. This was the upside of County and I was so pleased by the graciousness of most of the staff.

But I had also gained other insights into hospital medicine while at County that made a lasting impression on me. One insight came as I watched a woman, pregnant with her tenth baby, lying on a gurney waiting for her delivery room to be prepared. I heard a massive urge to push coming from the gurney so I ran over and pulled back her sheets. I was able to catch her baby before it fell to the floor. The staff praised me to the skies, not for saving the life of the child but for being able to deliver a baby without first putting on gloves. Seriously. They said, "You must have learned that from home birth!"

Section One: Homefirst Health Services

So, despite my excellent training at County, I was learning that the distortion in hospital medicine was so great that it was turning brilliant doctors into people who couldn't function anymore. They would have chosen to put on gloves and let the infant fall off the gurney. I was seeing the lack of wisdom in modern medicine which was negating so many of the potentially good things that could be done by it. I felt very fortunate to have a practice waiting for me that would for the most part remove me from these absurdities.

The Birthing Gurus

I finished my training at County and began to work with Dr. White. He was beginning to send me some cases of my own. At the same time, I was assisting Dr. Beatrice Tucker with the deliveries of her last few patients. She was a wonderful 81-year-old obstetrician. I had the feeling there wasn't anything she didn't know about birth. I still feel that way.

Dr. Tucker was America's first woman obstetrician and Director of the Chicago Maternity Center for fifty years. Under her supervision there were over 100,000 babies delivered at home with a safety record unsurpassed. Most of those babies were delivered to poor mothers who had no prenatal care, but who called the Maternity Center for help when they went into labor. Of course, this makes her safety record seem even more impressive! And these were days before blood banks and antibiotics.

When I met Dr. Tucker, she was closing the doors of

the Chicago Maternity Center due to lack of funds. It was 1973. I would go to her house every Tuesday night and discuss obstetrics with her. She was history and I was witnessing her last doctoring days. I just couldn't let go. I would go on these fascinating deliveries with her in her chauffeur-driven (due to her failing eye sight) yellow Volkswagen whenever I could. Twins, breech births, whatever there was to see and learn, I was there.

She was like a grandmother in the best sense of the word, inspiring confidence and security in the laboring women. A wise and dignified grandmother - much like my own. But that digression is for later.

In my chain of inspirational birthing teachers, I must mention the guru of all home birth gurus, Dr. Herbert Ratner. He trained all of us home birth doctors either directly or indirectly. Dr. Ratner, who recently passed away at the age of 90, was a philosopher and true pro-life parent. For inspiration in raising our own six children, my wife and I often attended his monthly forums on family life which he conducted well past his retirement. He was a general practitioner for years, a professor of philosophy at Loyola University and the teacher of Dr. White.

Dr. Ratner arranged to have his son-in-law, Dr George Dietz, spend time teaching me obstetrics on his day off when I was a resident at Cook County Hospital. Dr. Ratner was very influential in the founding of the La Leche League of experienced mothers who could be consulted on matters of breastfeeding.

Possibly one of Dr. Ratner's simplest and most profound thoughts is, "G-d is forgiving. Nature is not." He

explains that you can transgress against G-d and be for-
given. But nature doesn't forgive our mistakes. The mistakes made in modern high tech birth which illustrate
this point are numerous. We proponents of home birth
have seen time and time again that women are not
meant to give birth flat on their backs on a delivery
table. Modern women do not need drugs and episiotomies to do what their ancestors have been doing
naturally at home for centuries. But more about that in
the next chapters of this book.

I spent my career as a student looking for professors
who knew answers. These true teachers, Doctors
Ratner, White, Tucker, Mendelsohn and Peterson taught
me most of what I know. They taught me the truth. I
asked the same questions over and over of all these
teachers and their answers were remarkably the same -
not so much the specific answers but the way to get to
the answers, the way to bring children into the world
without transgressing against nature.

How can I ever thank my teachers? By becoming a
disciple of the birthing gurus? By writing a book about
what I have learned?

So, Why Me?

My digressing takes me full circle.
Why me?
How did I come to carry the home birth torch?
Was it the inspiration of my two grade school
friends? My negative experiences in medical school? The
wise teachers I pursued for information? The awful hos-

14

pital birth of my son? My wonderful wife knowing that there must be a better way to have children? Seeing the joys and safety of home birth firsthand?

One last digression may complete my answer.

Maybe it was my grandmother, the supreme lady of our house when I was growing up. The lady whose daughter at the tender age of 16 married my father . The lady who helped to raise my three brothers and me.

My father got a package deal when he married his young bride, a package deal he came to love. He felt so fortunate to have a family since his entire family was destroyed during Hitler's reign of terror in Europe. He would tell my grandmother that she was the reason his four sons would amount to something in life.

She did instill a strength and security in my brothers and me that has served us well. She taught us to value older people and to see that they had something special to offer. I am sure that she is a large part of the answer to, "Why me?"

She taught me to listen to what the great older doctors like Dr. Tucker and Dr. Ratner had to say. She taught me to value their experiences. She taught me that if I could learn from them, then I could carry the torch. I could pass on to others the best of what these sages had to offer the world.

I often say that there is nothing original in my practice. My home birth techniques are simply my best attempts to imitate the masters. And Grandma taught me that there is nothing wrong with that.

Scientifically Sound Birth

*"Most of the fundamental ideas of science
are essentially simple, and may, as a rule,
be expressed in a language
comprehensible to everyone."
— Albert Einstein,
The Evolution of Physics*

*M*y father, a Rabbi, used to tell a joke about the man who went to the doctor. The doctor gave him a prescription. He paid the doctor and took the prescription to the drug store. The pharmacist gave him his pills and he paid for them. As he was leaving the store, he passed a garbage can and threw away the pills. The pharmacist saw him and asked, "Why did you throw away your medicine?" The man replied, "I paid the doctor because he has to live. I paid you because you have to live. But I have to live too."

My father's joke is really very appropriate to the discussion of a positive medical philosophy. The man in the story had a very positive outlook. He asked his doctor for an opinion about a specific health matter but was too interested in his continued good health to take the prescribed medicine.

More of us should respond to the medical profession as did the man in my father's joke. Ninety percent of the time it does not help, and often deteriorates one's condition, to swallow the medicine and the advice of the modern doctor. Doctors are simply trained in a school of thought that says, "We treat illness. Treatment is better than no treatment." So they often reach into the large collection of pills and literature dumped on them by drug companies and "treat" patients with something a pharmaceutical sales representative said would be appropriate.

In my opinion, this is unscientific medicine coming from a negative philosophical base. This unscientific medicine is being practiced on virtually every person in this country with some very depressing results.

This unscientific system has even made it unsafe to give birth in this country. The U. S. has fallen to 24th place from its former 5th place as a safe country in which to have a baby. The unscientific medicine practiced at births over the past 30 years has plunged America to the dead-last position among the top industrial nations in numbers of healthy babies born to healthy mothers. This type of medical practice cannot, and must not, continue in this great country of ours.

Unscientific Medicine

Most people in the United States are trained by their doctors to view medicine as an indisputable science. Americans trust modern medicine quite literally "with their lives." Submitting to suggested treatments, tests and surgeries, and consuming quantities of prescribed medicines is something most people do without question. Doctors want consumers to believe that there are hard and fast rules being followed in their practices, scientific principles determining the best treatment for any given ailment. But there is a lot of unscientific medicine being practiced today.

To cite one example, according to a *Time* magazine medical report of April 25, 1988, some 19 billion diagnostic tests were performed by doctors in the U. S. last year. This is a rate of 80 tests for every man, woman and child in the country.

> "Critics charge that doctors, through greed, poor judgement or fear of malpractice suits, are ordering billions of dollars' worth of needless tests. Patients are willing accomplices, ever ready to put their faith in what appears to be scientific evidence. . . . Worse, owing to sloppy laboratory work or doctors' mistakes, the results are too often wrong or misinterpreted; thus they may actually harm patients by failing to detect serious diseases or by indicating illness when none exists."

Unnecessary testing is just one example of how medicine today has to be viewed more as a lucrative philosophical business than a humanitarian science. Patients are being treated according to the doctor's outlook on his work, not according to scientific laws. A doctor's philosophy will, of course, be reflected in his practice. Who wants to be the patient of a doctor who is operating out of greed, poor judgement or fear of malpractice? The actions of these doctors can and do place lives in jeopardy every day.

The same *Time* article goes on to say that

"some doctors may be ordering needless, but profitable, tests once they have purchased equipment for use in their own offices. 'More than 190,000 doctors, according to a Senate subcommittee, are doing some in-office testing.' Brochures from the manufacturers of equipment openly court the young doctor: 'In-office testing that helps build a nestegg,' reads one."

Most likely to be tempted to make money from testing, the article says are, " . . . younger, technology-minded doctors with huge medical school debts to pay off."

I do agree with the article's statement by Dr. Eleanor Travers, Director of Pathology for the U. S. Veterans Administration who says, "The more experience a physician has, the fewer the tests that should be necessary."

This is certainly true when it comes to caring for the

healthy pregnant women I see in my practice. Most tests are largely unnecessary and hazardous but profitable to the practitioner.

The obstetrical system in our country is no stranger to the unscientific method. Obstetrics, which is really a combined philosophy, business and religion, does not have science as its base. Obstetricians practice much more philosophy than science. Pregnant women are tested, medicated and operated on to excess every day by this profession in an unethical and dangerous way.

This unscientific medicine is dangerous to us as a nation. Our maternal and infant mortality rate is unacceptable for a society so sophisticated as ours. We produce more premature infants than any other country with our interventionist technology and then praise ourselves for saving some of their lives. Our record number of birth accidents each year is a puzzle to other developed societies such as Scandinavia, which has a large home birth practice.

When it comes to birth in the U. S., technological measures such as intravenous fluids, electronic monitoring, ultrasound, pitocin, and forceps are necessary only about 5% of the time, but they are applied virtually to every birth due to the modern obstetrician's orientation. The practice of interfering with most pregnancies and labors complicates matters and often damages or even kills mothers and their infants.

The American obstetrical system has failed us miserably. But I do feel that there is hope in this country. Americans have one virtue unsurpassed in the world. We are willing to admit mistakes. Educated parents of the 21st Century are opting away from the pseudo-science of obstetrics and the pseudo-safety of the hospital. They are choosing home birth and vaginal birth after cesarean sections.

We did make a mistake 50 years ago when the new field of obstetrics was allowed to flourish freely in the U.S. We are now in the process of correcting that mistake. We are taking a second look at birthing information that worked so well in the past and bringing that information into the present.

Scientific Literature Supports Natural Birth

Support for noninterventional birth abounds in the obstetricians' own modern scientific literature. Obstetrical literature is quite sound and well-researched. It is simply that obstetricians, for whatever reason, don't read or adhere to the findings of their own discipline. If they did then I would not have had to write this book to alert consumers and their infants.

For example, in the July, 1986 issue of *British Journal of Obstetrics and Gynecology*, Marjorie Tews discusses her research findings on obstetrical intervention in an article entitled "Do Obstetric Intranatal Interventions Make Birth Safer?"

> "Summary. Impartial analyses of the evidence from official statistics, national surveys and specific studies consistently find that perinatal mortality is much higher when obstetric intranatal interventions are used, as in consultant hospi-

tals, than when they are little used, as in unattached general practitioner maternity units and at home. The conclusion holds that after allowance has been made for the higher predelivery risk status of hospital births as a result of the booking and transfer policies. It holds even more strongly for births at high than at low predicted risk. It follows that the increased use of interventions, implied by increased hospitalization, could not have been the cause of the decline in the national perinatal mortality rate over the last 50 years and analysis of results by different methods confirms that the latter would have declined more in the absence of the former. Data are presented which point to the deleterious effect of interventions on the incidence of low birth weight and short gestation and their associated mortality. Also presented are data supporting the alternative explanation of the decline in perinatal mortality, namely the improvement in the health status of mothers built up over several generations. The organization of the maternity service stands indicted by the evidence. Despite the beliefs of those responsible, it has not promoted, and cannot promote, the objective of reducing perinatal mortality."

Many scientific reports such as this one (listed in the reference section at the back of this book) support home birth and show technological intervention to be harmful to mothers and infants. It must be explained that all U. S. hospitals are consultant hospitals, as referred to in this issue of the *British Journal of Obstetrics and Gynecology*, hospitals where the perinatal mortality was the highest. It was the small maternity hospitals which had the safer birth records due to little interference in the birthing process. There are none of these unattached, general practitioner maternity units in America, no small maternity hospitals run by general practitioners and midwives. There are no general practitioners either.

Despite many scientific reports such as this one, modern obstetricians continue to intervene excessively at births, to maintain their system of large consultant hospitals and to find home birth unthinkable.

It is frightening to realize that most hospital-trained obstetricians have never seen normal birth. Virtually every hospital birth today involves unnecessary intervention, a minimum of an episiotomy and IV fluids, and often forceps and painkilling drugs. These unwarranted procedures alter the dynamics of birth so much that unless a doctor has been to a home birth, he or she has never seen a truly normal labor and delivery.

And so it is that the obstetrician's philosophy sets the ball in motion for interventionist birth. Intervention gives power, control and credit to the doctors for birth itself. Many obstetricians have been known to say behind the scenes that they only feel they have "delivered" the baby when they perform a cesarean section. It is a powerful feeling to "deliver" babies rather than leaving delivery to the mothers themselves.

Physician Attended Home Birth and Its Philosophy

I have found it necessary for my medical staff to concentrate on the scientific study of birth since it is dangerous to mothers and infants to follow the American obstetrical model any longer. As a result we are a new breed of medical doctor, studying birth, following scientific principles and the dictates of nature. We follow a positive scientific philosophy which says that every child is a premium child. We see that children are born under the watchful eye of a physician who wishes to, in the words of Hippocrates, the father of medicine, "above all, do no harm."

A positive and scientific medical philosophy makes a large difference in how pregnant patients are treated by their doctors. We at Homefirst believe that pregnancy, labor and delivery are normal events, not pathological processes. We rely on these natural processes whenever possible, reserving operative interference and care for those cases where there is a probability of damage to the mother or baby without such interference. When the pregnant woman is treated by a physician who knows her chances of delivering a healthy baby are excellent, then she is empowered and confident about her body and her ability to give birth.

From a pregnant woman's initial visit to our offices till the day she delivers her baby, we stress to her our own credo about birth.

Section One: Homefirst Health Services

We tell her we believe:

1. that she can give birth.
2. that she can enjoy giving birth.
3. that she can give birth without drugs, epi-siotomies, forceps or c-section surgery.
4. that she can have a most enjoyable and safe experience giving birth at home.
5. that she can successfully breast-feed her baby.
6. that she can give birth vaginally even if she has had a previous c-section delivery.
7. that we can work together to make America the safest place in the world to give birth.

The doctors who taught me about home birth understood that mothers, not doctors, deliver babies. Their actions reinforced this belief at every delivery. When my great teachers, Doctors Ratner, Tucker and White, would enter the homes of laboring women, a tremendous feeling of warmth and confidence would blanket the whole family. They entered homes quite literally as "lifeguards" for the mothers and babies.

Lifeguards never pull competent swimmers out of the water while they are swimming but are ever vigilant should the swimmers find themselves in distress.

These great doctors knew what they were doing. They brought to the homes the belief that mothers could give birth. They "warmed up" the families for the big event, in a sense, by making everyone feel comfortable with what was going to happen.

I try to emulate their actions at every birth because this is such an important aspect of safe birth. The Homefirst physician's faith in women as birth givers can make the difference between normal delivery and cesarean section.

This can be contrasted with the hospital belief that birth is a pathological event. The hospital staff wants the pregnant woman, at her moment of greatest vulnerability, to respect them and their wishes with a blatant disregard for her needs. They want her to accommodate them: stay in bed, don't eat or drink, don't walk around and leave all supportive family members in the waiting room until the baby is born.

It is the job of our staff members to accommodate the laboring woman, to see that the home environment is conducive to giving birth. Our doctors and nurses arrive with a positive outlook, their vans loaded with over 100 pieces of modern technological equipment to set up a zone of safety for the laboring mother. They carefully monitor her progress without interfering with labor and give the family encouragement and input as to what is happening. It is the goal of the medical team to provide continuous medical support and supervision so that progress will continue.

One woman, who delivered her baby under the watchful eye of Dr. Beatrice Tucker, said, "She was like a favorite grandmother in the best sense of the word. She brought warmth, professionalism and a comfort that couldn't be matched."

It is often a surprise to a newly trained doctor, observing home birth, to see how little, it may appear, that the home birth doctor does. In contrast to hospital deliveries where the staff is busily calling for monitors, needles, IV tubes, catheters and scissors, the home birth doctor's chief role is that of a careful observer, and as such he or she is doing plenty.

Our doctors' skills lies in their abilities to distinguish between the problem and non-problem cases. One of my staff doctors commented that he is proud to "do" so little at a home birth. "It means that I have helped provide a safe and comfortable atmosphere where nature can take over and do its job."

On this point Dr. Tucker once said to me, "In the hospital they feel that if something is being 'done,' then you are getting your money's worth. But delivering a baby at home is much more work. You use your judgement to evaluate the home cases. At home you must have a highly qualified doctor present."

"Less is more," we believe. I tell the young doctors training in my practice that as a home birth practitioner you have to overcome the feeling that you have to always take action. Most of the time you don't. Nature will handle the progress of labor if the medical staff works to maintain that calm, protective zone for the mother. This zone is the doctor's prime concern - not the disturbing of nature's timetable with drugs, forceps and incisions.

Our doctors with their positive scientific philosophy have faith in nature. "A watchful expectancy" in the birthing situation, to use a phrase of the father of modern obstetrics, Dr. Joseph B. DeLee, is the most positive action the doctor can take. Proper scientific technique applied at home birth enables the physician to continuously supervise over 95% of births without having to resort to advanced intervention to bring about safe delivery. Non-interference gives everyone the best chance of having the most positive results in home birth.

Institution vs. Family

I have found no one who writes today about the demise of the American family has explored the negative impact of hospital birth. I believe that the decision to have an institutional hospital birth is at the heart of the destruction of American family life. The family starts with birth, and home birth traditionally was a cornerstone of strength in a family's life. Hospital birth deprives the new family of this most primal and strengthening experience.

In 1920, when birth was leaving the home and entering the hospitals in the U. S., there was an outcry. People didn't like it. There was a rise in infant and maternal mortality in the hospital. But control of birth, medical schools and hospitals were in the hands of powerful and wealthy families like the Rockefellers and the Morgans. It was in the best interest of their financial empires to influence the move of laboring women to hospitals. A major study as early as 1933 showed that hospital births were not as safe as home births.

It seems inevitable that if families are strong in a society, then the institutions are weak; and if the institutions are strong, then families are weak. Our

Section One: Homefirst Health Services

American institutional way of life is firmly implanted. Our families have been weakened by powerful economic and political forces most interested in perpetuating themselves.

You don't find people these days who will tell you that they were happy with the hospital births of their children. They may be pleased to leave the hospital with their new babies but at best describe the hospital experience as necessary if one wants a baby.

It is never described as an emotionally uplifting moment, not as the greatest day in their lives, not as the happening that brought them closer than ever before, but as a necessary experience if you want to have a baby. Hospital birth is something new mothers try to forget quickly. A mother who wants to have another hospital birth in the future has to block the experience from her mind in order to have the courage to go through the experience another time. The hospital is a necessary experience only if one knows of no other way of having a baby.

Institutional childbirth will never be a joyous experience because institutions do not aim to please any of the families they serve. They aim to perpetuate their own existence. In the U. S. the goal of hospitals is to ensure that you feel dependent on them. This dependent feeling guarantees that you will call on the institution again and again. The hospital will step in to weaken your family's strength. They will deliver your baby, direct the care and feeding of your baby, cure your illnesses, take care of your elderly family members for you and manage your death. And they extract a great price, personal and financial, for their services.

If an institution can control the beginning
family life, the birth of your first child, then they can
control everything else in your life. They "help" you
decide on institutional formula feedings for your baby;
institutional day care, maybe even from birth; institutional schooling beginning at a very early age; institutional careers to which your children may aspire; even
the institutional care of anyone in your family who is
sick or dying.

In contrast, "family thinking" brings questions and
problems back to the family to solve rather than taking
them to the institution. Dr. Robert Mendelsohn, one of
America's leading pediatricians, used to say that one
grandmother was worth two pediatricians. Families can
provide their own "in-house" birthing rooms, child care
systems, educational opportunities and care of the sick
and dying.

The Wellness of Birth

No one these days who has chosen an institutional
way of life for themselves and their family members
seems very happy with his or her decision. I have
noticed that those members of our society who have the
greatest emotional sense of well-being are those who
begin family life with a home birth and nurse their
babies.

The emotional experience of home birth changes
those involved in so many ways and for the rest of their
lives. It gives them a bond and a confidence that no one

can take away. One father said, "Having a baby at home makes your house a holy place." My mentor Dr. Beatrice Tucker once said of the home birth experience, "Home birth has an excitement lacking in the hospital. There is the excitement of the doctor coming into your home. It is uplifting. It is impossible not to feel the joy in the family."

My staff of Homefirst physicians and nurses come into homes bringing permission for the mothers to give birth. We give them the confidence to have their babies without drugs and unnecessary interventions. We are trusted by the families we treat much as general practitioners were many years ago. We do what we promised to do for the laboring couple, bringing no surprises or unexpected changes in their birth plan, unless, of course, something unusual arises in the course of labor.

Mothers at home are able to relax knowing they won't have to fight against us to have their babies. They are able to let go of all tensions and direct their energies towards delivery. This makes birth a joyful, not a fearful, event. Mothers at home are emotionally well. They can express their feelings and their needs in labor. They can most easily give birth in the atmosphere of love and concern carefully prepared for them by their friends, family and the Homefirst staff.

In the hospital community the emotional and psychological aspects of birth do not matter since they cannot be weighed, measured or tested with equipment. The family's sense of emotional well-being is not considered as a factor in hospital birth.

So emotional wellness becomes an added bonus at

home birth. At home it is so appropriate, so right that everyone contributes to the physical and emotional wellness of the new family. Who would not want such a wonderful addition to their birth experience if they knew they could choose it for themselves? Birth at home is so unique an experience that it cannot be explained. Only the witnessing of a home birth can explain the feeling, that terrific uplifting of spirits that occurs every time a new life is born into a couple's own home.

No matter how you approach home birth, it always works best — from a medical angle, a psychological angle, an emotional angle, a wellness angle and a spiritual angle. Those who choose it are privileged to have one of the most inspirational experiences of a lifetime.

This sense of emotional wellness which begins at birth leads home birth families to make other noninstitutional decisions together. In the best interest of the family, many of them choose to have a large number of children, operate home schools, work independently of institutions and to care for their elderly at home. These family decisions make them better able to cherish each new life and to live happier lives together.

Would You Have A Home birth?

I have found no other question as powerful in determining a person's belief system as this, "Would you consider having a home birth?"

More than any other question, this one demands an answer from the core of one's philosophical beliefs. People answer in one of three ways. Some people easily accept the idea of home birth, others say they might consider it if they found it to be safe, and a third group would never consider a home birth. These responses generally put people in one of two groups. The first two responses are from people who trust in God or nature, distrust the obstetrical system and have a tremendous love of family as the primary concern in their lives. The third response is from people who distrust God or nature, put their stock in man and technology, and put other priorities above family, such as careers or personal interests.

These are generalized polarities, of course, but the way people answer the home birth question does say a lot about them. A *Time* magazine article entitled "The Dilemmas of Childlessness", May 2, 1988 tends to support my personal findings about those who put other priorities above family. It states that 25% of college educated working women between 35 and 45 are childless. Those women who are not having children tend to be well-educated, live in urban areas, marry late and work outside the home; as a group they are not actively religious.

The article goes on to say,

. . . Society is accepting childlessness, but some women question whether they have violated a biological law.

Even those who choose to have no children at all seem to fall statistically in my second group, the group which has put other priorities above family. People from this group who hear me speak always ask, "But what if something goes wrong? What if I need intervention?" They just can't imagine trusting in their own bodies to perform without the aid of technology. It is almost as if they have shut off their natural instincts to operate in an institutional society. But as the *Time* article says, some of those childless by choice still sometimes feel they have violated nature's laws by making their institutional choices.

The readers of this book who feel they are respectful of nature but had hospital births are part of a growing third group I have not discussed, but a group I feel will appreciate this book. They are a group of believers in nature's ways whom obstetricians have scared into being technological thinkers by bombarding them with fear and guilt. The obstetrician's warning, "You should turn things over to a specialist just in case something goes wrong," can carry a lot of weight unless families are prepared to study the scientific facts of childbirth on their own. I hope to present those facts to families who have some doubts about the thinking of the obstetrical establishment.

Defying Modern Obstetrics

An example of institutional obstetrics became apparent to me when I was consulting with Maria, a pregnant woman considering a home birth. She and her husband came to me late in her pregnancy, after being alarmed that, in their church congregation, about 66% of the mothers were having their babies by cesarean section.

At this same time, her own obstetrician told her that she stood about a 50% chance of needing a cesarean section for delivery. There were no health problems indicating that this surgery might be needed. The doctor was simply telling her what her chances were with obstetrical care today.

This just didn't feel right to her since she was a perfectly healthy person. She had to defy modern medicine, leave her obstetrician towards the end of her pregnancy and go in search of an alternative that would guarantee her a good chance of not having a surgical delivery.

Fortunately for Maria, she did choose to have a home birth with no interventions and she had a healthy baby. But it was in her hands to do the researching to find a safe way to give birth. On her own Maria had to break away from institutional thought and find a medical practice employing a true scientific method and having a positive philosophy about birth.

In our quest to embrace high tech science in our society, we aren't really embracing science at all. The 66% cesarean statistic from Maria's church congregation says that. It was the philosophical decisions of these women's obstetricians to give them cesarean section surgery, not a scientific fact that they all needed surgery.

Positive Birthing Principles

It seems so ironic that the simple, yet sophisticated, method of having a baby at home can be one of the

answers to lowering the infant and maternal mortality
rate in this technological age. But it makes sense that
the secret to lowered mortality isn't anything new or
technologically advanced. Mother Nature herself prescribed home birth for us and her ways haven't
changed. Medicine just can't improve on what was originally intended for our bodies.

My staff and I are still following the sound principles
of obstetrics outlined by Dr. Beatrice Tucker over 50
years ago. Our system is not new. Time just hasn't
changed the effectiveness of Dr. Tucker's principles
which respect nature's plan for birth.

As the Director of the Chicago Maternity Center
from 1932 until 1972, over 100,000 babies were delivered safely at home under Dr. Tucker's direction. These
babies of Chicago's indigent mothers were born into the
city's most humble homes with a safety record unsurpassed in the country. At a time before blood banks and
antibiotics, Dr. Tucker was able to have such a record
due to her safe obstetrical practices. Her high standards
and positive philosophy made birth safe even in
Chicago's poorest neighborhoods.

By listening to Dr. Tucker and by accompanying her
to as many deliveries as I could, I concluded that her
home birth principles have never been surpassed for
safety.

The following were her eleven principles:
1. *A trained doctor must be completely in charge
   of the birth.*
2. *The mother should have adequate prenatal*

care.

3. Doctors and nurses must be in constant attendance at the labor.

4. The medical staff must have adequate equipment with them in the home.

5. The doctors must employ simple, intensive, aseptic technique.

6. The laboring mother must be in a favorable environment, her own home.

7. There should be a minimum of operative intervention in the birthing process. Less than 1% of the babies should be born by cesarean section.

8. Good hospitals should be available as back ups for the doctors delivering babies at home.

9. Doctors should take action early in the event of hemorrhage and know proper hemorrhage control.

10. There should be no interference permitted in the third stage of labor.

11. No pitocin should be used until after the birth of the baby. If any doctor disregards this rule, he should be dismissed from the practice.

"Any home birth service, of course, must be complemented by hospital services," Dr. Tucker added. "The two working hand in hand can do much to lower maternal mortality and the cost of obstetrical care."

No one knew more about birth than Dr. Tucker, due to her vast experience and wisdom. Application of her principles across the country, today, would be followed by a marked decrease in the maternal death rate.

It could be so simple to place the U. S. at the top of the list of countries where birth is a safe and healthy experience. No better system than Dr. Tucker's has ever been implemented. A look into the past at her excellent techniques could lead America to a healthy future.

A Message From My Mentor

The following dialogue is excerpted from an interview with the late Dr. Robert Mendelsohn, my teacher and mentor from medical school. Dr. Mendelsohn was one of the country's leading pediatricians, a medical maverick who authored several books on the dangers of modern medical practices. He was a great believer in my home birth practice and discussed it briefly in this excerpted interview with Dave Ormesher of Channel 38 Television in Chicago.

I have included this excerpt because Dr. Mendelsohn expresses better than anyone the difference between home and hospital birth.

Mendelsohn: Home birth (as it is practiced by Dr. Eisenstein and his staff) is not noninterventional. They intervene to protect the mother from obstetricians, the baby from pediatricians, and to protect both from the hospital. I regard that as interventionist.

Interviewer: Do you see a future for Family Practice? (Dr. Eisenstein's home birth practice.)

Mendelsohn: Hospitals are going out of business.

Obstetricians are giving up their practices.
People will be left with only one alternative,
home birth at the hands of home birth doctors
and midwives. This is far safer than (being in
the hands of) obstetricians in
hospitals.Interviewer: How is Family Practice
(Dr. Eisenstein's practice) different from main
line (obstetrical) practices?

Mendelsohn: They (Dr. Eisenstein and his staff)
don't endanger mothers and babies with dangerous drugs, tests and surgeries. Your chances
of death, disability, mental retardation, epilepsy,
convulsions and sudden infant death syndrome
(SIDS) are far greater in the hospital than at
home. If obstetricians are giving drugs to
women in labor, doing episiotomies, and have a
high rate of cesarean sections, then they are no
good.

We need a suspicion of that which is modern to
reaffirm that which is traditional. Modern medicine tries
to scare people of diseases. I try to scare them of the
treatments. Regarding birth, doctors try to threaten parents that if you try to perform the "sacrament" of birth
outside of the "temple" (hospital), which I call the
Temple of Doom, then they will die and their babies will
die.

Modern medicine has a death orientation, not a life
orientation. The mortality rate drops around the world
during a doctors' strike when doctors are not practicing.

The Home Court Advantage

3

> *"Never does nature say one thing*
> *and wisdom another."*
> *— Decimus Juniaus Juvenal, Satires*

The Home Court Advantage in childbirth is my favorite topic, you know.

The expression "home court advantage" puts into words something I had struggled for years to explain about my home birth practice. Through twenty-six years and 14,000 safe home deliveries, one of the most popular questions asked of me continues to be, "What makes home birth safe?"

The safety issue is something I have always felt at a gut level and something explainable through statistical data. But I had been looking for years for an analogy to explain that special edge which all home birth mothers have over their hospital counterparts.

The answer came one Sunday afternoon. I was watching a football game on television. The sports announcer was analyzing the game and predicting the winner. This particular commentator would tell the listening audience minutes before the games who was going to win and lose. He looked at sports the way they should be examined, from a statistical standpoint. He said of his own heart surgery that he knew his chances were good. His doctor had told him he had a 15 to 1 chance of leaving the hospital alive.

People looked to this announcer to answer the question, "What is going to happen?" His way of predicting the answer was very interesting to me. He used a very large board to analyze the games. He would give the teams check marks in boxes on the board for their strengths in various categories, such as for having a strong quarterback or an outstanding fullback.

The last box on the board was reserved for the location of the game. If all else seemed equal, he would place a check mark in Chicago's box, for instance, saying, "I think Chicago will win because they are playing in Soldier Field. They have the home court advantage."

Those of us listening at home would be thinking, "You are a genius! Of course, Chicago will win."

I had listened to this announcer many times but all of a sudden I said, "He's right! Home birth has the home court advantage!"

It is something you can't buy with technology, with sophistication. I had finally found my analogy between sports and home birth. You can pick up the newspaper any day and clearly see that the home teams win at home with a high frequency. Even the statistics available from the most recent Winter Olympics show that the U.S. has won the most medals in Olympic games held in the U.S.

It is interesting that basketball has the greatest home court advantage, possibly because the fans sit the closest to the players. As the arena gets larger and the fans get further away, the advantage is not as pronounced. Basketball is followed in advantage by baseball and then by football, where the fans are the furthest away from the playing field.

It is no surprise that similar statistics apply to having a baby in your own "home court." Babies are born at home usually in half the time of a hospital-delivered baby and usually with no intervention from the home birth team. The mother has her "fans" there, as close as they can get to her and as many fans as she needs around her to "cheer" her to victory.

As I thought more about the home court advantage, I remembered my own high school basketball days. We had a unique court advantage. One of the baskets was one foot lower than the other. We would try to get the visiting team to shoot first at the lower basket. Then after halftime when we switched baskets it was a guarantee that their first shots would be a foot too short. Now, that was really a home court advantage!

Home court advantage is a rather magical thing. How does one describe it in professional sports where every court is measured to the last millimeter, every player playing at peak performance? The home court advantage works the same way for the pros as it did for our high school team. It is a very real thing. When a team walks onto an opposing team's field, they have certain disadvantages that make it difficult for them to win even if they possess the same or superior skills.

Soon after I came across this analogy for myself, a patient who happened to be a veterinarian further reinforced it for me. When he came to see me, he told me a story about delivering some puppies. One of the family dogs was ready to give birth. She was carrying eight puppies. The first four came out just fine, my patient related. But at this point he moved the mother dog to another location and her labor came to a complete stop.

He was preparing to give the dog some medication to start labor again and was actually considering having to do a c-section delivery of the last four puppies. There was one last thing to try first. The family moved the dog back to the location she had originally chosen for the delivery of her offspring. In a short time labor began again and the last four puppies were born with no problem.

As with the mother dog, the advantage of giving birth in one's own home court can be translated as the difference between having a c-section and a natural delivery. Choosing one's own comfortable surroundings for delivery can make all the difference for humans too.

An inordinate number of cesarean section deliveries are occurring in our nation's hospitals. I really believe the sights, smells and sounds of the hospital complicate labor as it did for my patient's family pet. It is those complications which lead to unnecessary surgeries.

I don't think it means we have poor doctors and nurses in our hospitals. In fact, we have some of the finest doctors in the world. But our doctors and nurses

44

working in the hospitals lose one very strong advantage — the home court advantage.

Can Hospitals Be Made Safe For Birth?

If I could change the hospital and somehow make it as safe as home for laboring women, would I do it? I'd argue, "No." There is something about just walking into a hospital that changes the dynamics of labor. Under any circumstances labor time is doubled in the hospital. If you put any woman in the hospital, her labor will slow down or stop because her hormonal balance has changed. Her energies have to go into dealing with her strange surroundings, not into the birth itself.

When the mother has been in labor for a reasonable amount of time at the hospital, the doctors want to interfere with the course of things. However, they themselves have changed normal labor into abnormal labor by prolonging it in this strange environment. The reasonable amount of labor didn't deliver the baby so now they feel they must intervene to get the baby out.

Many interventions such as drugs, intravenous fluids, electronic monitoring and forceps come in the hours of labor that wouldn't have existed at home. Hospitals that allow you to labor naturally for the first ten hours won't allow you to labor naturally for the next ten hours. At home these next ten are spent getting to know the already delivered baby, not trying to push the baby out. In other words, hospitals create the problems of delivery and then obstetricians have to try to solve them.

Home births occur before the miserable second half

of hospital labor has a chance to start. Home births occur before problems happen. If women knew that most of them could have half as much labor and no complications, they would all be choosing home birth!

Prior to this century, birth always took place in the comfort of home with close friends and family surrounding the mother. Giving birth requires privacy and intimacy, as does the sexuality between man and woman. Birth is a very sexual and personal experience. A warm and intimate environment allows us to function as we were intended to. It is really a very basic instinct that we have lost touch with in the United States.

Is Home Birth Scientifically Sound?

We home birth doctors often get labeled as unscientific. We are pictured as hippie leftovers from the 1960s or practitioners of some dangerous cult which tortures women and babies. However, we are very scientific and we want to see technology applied correctly.

Modern technology is being applied inappropriately at most hospital births today producing disastrously long labors, birth accidents and poor bonding opportunities for mothers and babies. This is unacceptable. A scientifically-oriented doctor works as an instrument for preserving the safety of the birthing process.

A frequently asked question regarding the safety of my practice is, "What does the medical establishment think of having babies at home?"

I can only answer that question indirectly by citing the scientific literature published by the medical establishment. Traditional establishment medical journals reinforce over and over again the safety of our home birth practices. In fact, the obstetrician is the one not following the recommendations of his own professional journals.

For example, in obstetrical journals and other current publications my staff and I recently found 162 articles supporting our findings that a vaginal birth is much safer than another c-section for someone who has had a previous cesarean section delivery. However, only 7% of women are being given a chance by their doctors to have a vaginal delivery.

Examples of this kind abound. From modern establishment scientific literature one also learns that there is no need, in low risk women, for measures such as monitors, IV fluids, ultrasound, episiotomies and the traditional position for hospital labor and delivery, namely, the woman flat on her back in bed. Over 90% of all pregnant women are low risk and they are all being treated as high-risk by modern obstetricians.

One grossly overused procedure is electronic fetal monitoring. According to a recent article in Ob. Gyn. News, the American College of Obstetricians and Gynecologists (ACOG) might soon reverse its guidelines on the use of electronic fetal monitoring in high-risk pregnancies. The cover story of Ob. Gyn. News, volume 23, number 9, states that ACOG's committee on obstetrics has recommended to the ACOG executive board that "periodic auscultation be an acceptable alternative to electronic fetal monitoring for high-risk pregnancies." Auscultation is the listening to fetal heart tones with the use of a head stethoscope on the mother's abdomen.

In the words of Dr. Harold Schulman, a member of the obstetrics committee and Chief of Obstetrics at Winthrop University Hospital, Mineola, N.Y., "We had come to terms with the accumulating literature showing that fetal monitoring was not only not superior (to auscultation) but may even be dangerous." The article goes on to say that none of eight studies involving nearly 50,000 pregnant women "demonstrated any benefit of fetal monitoring and the results of five indicated that women who were electronically monitored were more likely to undergo cesarean section than those who were not."

One more case to be made about unnecessary routine fetal monitoring lies in its use of ultrasound. Ultrasound waves actually raise the temperature of the unborn baby, and we just don't know the impact on such small bodies. This technique should be applied only to cases where a problem is strongly suspected, not to predict delivery dates and certainly not to show the mother a first "picture" of her baby. Nature determines the optimal date for the baby's birthday, not an inaccurate technological device which can be off by weeks.

Routine ultrasound, I believe, will soon be discovered as unsafe as x-ray was found to be after all pregnant women had been routinely x-rayed in the 1940s. These x-rays resulted in untold cases of cancer across the country.

I could spend many chapters elaborating on the inappropriateness of routine technological measures used on pregnant women. Let it suffice to say that routine use of these measures is unfounded and many times dangerous. Maybe the most important point I can make is that consumers can verify my findings for themselves in medical literature. I would like to let couples know that they too could research the safety of various tests and explore birthing options for themselves in current obstetrical literature.

All major medical libraries have internet access. Anyone can research a topic such as "ultrasound" or "episiotomy" or "cesarean section" and find many, many articles to read on the advisability of avoiding these techniques if at all possible. You may also refer to our Homefirst Web page (http://www.homefirst.com) for further sources. You will find much support in these articles for the majority of women giving birth in a noninterventionist way. This is simply the best way for most women to deliver their babies.

Women Can Enjoy Giving Birth

Laboring at home is not only a nice and safe experience. Women laboring at home actually enjoy giving birth. The home environment just doesn't allow labor to progress in an abnormal fashion. The mothers are surrounded by familiar sights, smells, and foods, and people who care about them. No one has to worry about which unfamiliar people will be walking in or what they will be doing to them to alter the progress of labor. Often as soon as the baby is born, the parents are ready to consider having another baby. How often is this heard after a hospital birth?

49

Section One: **Homefirst Health Services**

Modern childbirth classes teach the husband to fight for his wife and baby's best interests during delivery. But a husband is always placed in a dilemma at a hospital birth. How could he possibly know how to fight against an entire medical staff making recommendations for fetal monitors, drugs, or even cesarean sections? One of the nicest things about home as a birth setting is that husbands don't have to have their guard up. They don't have to fight to have basic good scientific technique applied to their wive's labors and deliveries. At home, everyone's energy can go into the birth, not into a fight about the principles of safe birth.

Prenatal Care in the Scientifically Sound Birth System

The trust families have in our Homefirst staff is trust that has been earned during pregnancy. Husbands and wives have come to know that our doctors and nurses will keep their promises about birth, that whatever decisions are made in labor and delivery are in the best interest of the mother and baby. This is a tremendously comforting feeling both during pregnancy and delivery.

We believe a prenatal visit is not adequate if the mother is simply weighed, measured and examined for fetal heart tones. Of course, these procedures are necessary, but they aren't procedures which promote continued good health.

It is the role of the home birth doctors to create a caring atmosphere from the beginning of pregnancy to

50

help make families feel positive about their expected child. We share in the families' feelings of excitement about birth and we are delighted in our role of helping to bring new life into our expectant families' homes. These shared feelings become the prime motivation for the continued good health of the pregnant mother.

At prenatal visits it is our desire to establish and strengthen an old-fashioned trust between the doctor and expectant family, the kind of trust patients used to place in the family's general practitioner who knew them well and often treated patients in their own homes.

This type of trust maintains health in a way prenatal tests and measures never could. It also makes the future labor and delivery go faster and smoother because the family knows there is nothing suspect about the doctors and their methods. As we promise, no unnecessary interventions are done in the family's home. The Homefirst doctor will arrive with the prime goal of maintaining a safe and comfortable atmosphere for the laboring mother. This establishes an emotional wellness within the family most conducive to safe birth.

A grandfather, who was attending one of my Sunday night home birth seminars, expressed it better than I ever could. He was there with his two daughters, both of them pregnant. One of his daughters had had a child at home previously and now both daughters were scheduled for home births.

Their father got up and said, "I love what Homefirst Health Services is doing. I believe the emotional wellness of home birth that you talk about is the same as love. It is the outpouring of the love your doctors and nurses have for their patients that makes a difference. That love causes the release of medicines in the laboring women that science hasn't even found yet — medicines that make things go well at home."

We have to look to "new," but really ancient, birthing techniques in our country to return America to being a safe birthing place. It is time to take a look at doctors like myself and those in my practice and at our scientific techniques. It is time to reexamine our own culture's birthing history.

Chicago, itself, is rich in home birth history. The Chicago Maternity Center doctors worked for seventy-five years on Maxwell Street delivering babies at home with an unsurpassed safety record in America. It is time to examine the techniques of countries which have excellent safety records for delivery of infants and the health of mothers and babies. Interestingly enough, countries at the top of the list are those with a large home birth component, as in most of the Scandinavian countries.

Who Has Home Births These Days?

In the 1990s an interesting aspect of the home birth trend is that middle and upper income families are opting for home birth, not the indigent families of the 1920s and 1930s who had no options. Certainly the statistics of The Chicago Maternity Center have proven that all people should consider home birth regardless of education or income. Homefirst is currently making concerted efforts toward being able to provide this option to all women.

The trend of today, however, is that well-read and well-educated families are looking into our "new" idea of home birth because they are discovering that it is safer. They are disturbed by what modern obstetrical practices have been doing to women and babies and are learning about alternatives for themselves. Anyone who does some investigating of his or her own does not want to be a part of the alarming statistics related to hospital birth.

Most of my home birth families are college graduates. Many of the mothers are nurses themselves and many of the fathers are employed in high tech positions. They are people who understand the importance and safety of the natural birth process. They realize that giving birth is hard work which is best performed in accordance with the laws of nature. They believe that for this reason alone birth must happen at home. If it were simply a mechanical process, then the hospital would be a good enough alternative location.

This brings me back to the home court advantage. I recently heard an interview with a local teaching hospital obstetrician who said that almost every day at the hospital there is a birth that starts out absolutely normal and something goes awry. She said that is why one can't have a baby at home.

In my practice we believe just the opposite, almost every birth starts out normal; and if something goes awry, we do everything we can to keep it normal. Our goal is to maintain normalcy. The home birth families have their own comfortable surroundings and most of all a support team of their own choosing, family and friends, to keep things normal for them. This obstetrician proves my point about the safety of home birth when she says hospital births start out normal and then something goes wrong. I agree with her 100%!

To illustrate the point of keeping things normal, consider the case of the grumpy husband returning home after a horrible day at work. In one scenario the husband complains loudly to his wife upon entering their home, "I just had the most miserable day of my life!" His wife fires back, "I did too!" And the two begin to play a one-upmanship game about how bad things are. Suddenly blood pressures are up and everything begins to go wrong.

In another scenario the husband complains, "I just had the most miserable day of my life!" His wife responds, "But it is over now and we are together again." In this case, the husband's blood pressure returns to normal and health abounds at this household.

Modern obstetrics is similar to the husband and wife yelling at one another. The laboring woman yells, "This is terrible!" The hospital obstetrical team yells back, "And it is going to get worse!"

Home birth is like the second case. The laboring woman yells, "This is terrible!" and the family responds, "Yes, but we are here to help you. We know you can do it and soon we will see the new baby."

Personal Perspectives

The following are testimonial call-ins excerpted from

The Homefirst Family Health Forum radio program. They are calls from parents who have had home births themselves. They called me at the radio station to support the notion of the home court advantage from their personal perspectives.

Kim, a Homefirst Health Services nurse:

I'm calling in from a home in Romeoville where I am with a family which had a new baby last night. I'd like to describe the home court advantage from my perspective right now.

As I look around the living room I see the mother, sister and older children of the new mother all here in her cheering section. These family members were here last night and came back again this morning to see how things are going.

The mother, Caroline, has had both hospital and home births. Her labors are never easy, but the hospital labors were 24 hours and this home birth was 12 hours. For this home birth Caroline spent much of the labor time in her living room. She told me it helped her to concentrate and have more control over things to be there with her family. She didn't go into the bedroom till ten minutes before the baby was born.

Most home birth mothers don't spend much time in the bedroom. They just go there to push out the baby. Caroline delivered on her hands and knees with her husband supporting her. When it was time she told her husband, "Go get the children!" Caroline's mother commented this morning, "I wish I could have had my babies this way."

Caroline commented that this baby's temperament seems calmer than her other children's temperaments were at birth. Also she had had a bleeding problem after her hospital births but not this time. Home birth mothers rarely bleed excessively because their hormone levels are high after the exhilarating experience of giving birth without drugs. You would never know that she had a baby last night because some of the workers from Caroline's own business are here already and she is now in the living room conducting business.

Dr. Steve, the attending doctor, on the same delivery:

Caroline's labors are a little longer than usual, but it is certainly no coincidence that her hospital deliveries were twice as long as her home birth. There is no question that the home court advantage speeded things up this time. It made drugs unnecessary and the family support gave her something that drugs never could, that extra energy to manage labor and deliver a healthy baby.

Caroline's labor exemplifies a statement made by the father of modern obstetrics, Dr. Joseph B. DeLee. He said, "The most important skill of the low risk specialist is watchful expectancy."

Birth is a normal process. To maintain a little to no interference with the process is the best guide for doctors and midwives. But constant watchfulness is essential.

Caroline's labor was ideal for extreme intervention had she been in any hospital in this country. She had had false labor one week before the baby actually was born. However, I evaluated her case and determined that there was no problem for either the mother or the baby. If she had gone into a hospital, she would have had all kinds of interference as drastic as pitocin or even a cesarean section.

It was shown by her normal delivery that the baby's real birthday was a week away from the first contractions. In a case like this, the presence of the presence of the family goes beyond words. They give spiritual and emotional support to the mother and then, when the baby is born, they receive in return that spiritual uplift that comes when a new life is born into the world. There is nothing like it!

Marguerete is the mother of seven. She has had five hospital births and two home births. Gail, her oldest child, was there for the birth of her baby brother at home and subsequently has had her own baby at home.

Marguerete commented:
My five hospital births each required

about 24 hours of labor. When I called Dr. Eisenstein to come to the house for the first of our home births, he was there in no time. I remember apologizing to him and explaining that it would be a long time before he would be needed. He told us that it would be soon simply because we were at home this time. We were all amazed when the baby was born shortly thereafter.

For my first baby I was strapped down. I couldn't move, was forced to have an enema and received gas for the actual delivery. I kept stretching my neck to see the baby afterwards. The nurses wouldn't let me hold her till she was cleaned up and then they didn't want me to unwrap her to get a good look and feel of my first child.

All these restrictions played a part in my hospital labors being so long. We were so happy to discover that there was an alternative to this. I said to my husband, "Here we are in our mid-thirties, we have five children, and we have never shared a birth together." Our home births were wonderful!

Gail, Marguerete's daughter, saw Dr. Eisenstein again when she was in her own early stages of pregnancy. He commented that he had once taken care of someone who looked very much like her.

Gail:

That was my mother you took care of!

There was never any doubt that I could deliver a baby at home. My mother did it and I knew I could do it. If I had any questions in pregnancy or during labor, I could turn to Mom because she knew what it was like to be going through all this. I had no fears and no doubts about home birth because of my mom.

The Exhilaration Of Birth Can Be Handed Down

Traditionally, mothers have passed on to their daughters the secrets of home birth and experienced it as the most joyful time in life. These days mothers pass on to their daughters that hospital birth will surely be an unpleasant experience.

The exhilaration of birth can be passed down from generation to generation. Witnessing a birth makes you feel so wonderful. There is a special intensity about it all and there is no better labor coach for any woman than her own mother. She can say to her daughter with confidence, "You can do it!"

My hope and prayer is that every young woman in the future can be as fortunate as Gail in being able to call her mother when she goes into labor — a mother who can so skillfully help her to give birth as it has been done at home for many, many years.

Suggestions From Callers For Comfortable Labor

The following advice on how to have a more comfortable and easy labor comes from experienced home birth parents who called in to The Homefirst Family Health Forum.

> *Louise:* A mental attitude of just letting it happen helps tremendously. I had two fast births at home. If I felt discomfort, I would focus my attention on putting out energy. I would send out love energy to my husband. It became a feeling of expansion — not pain. This made giving birth a terrific high.

> *Kim, a Homefirst nurse:* Don't forget water comforts in labor. Take baths and showers and stay well hydrated. Drink frozen fruit juice chips or chew on crushed ice.

> *Amy:* My mother was here for my son's birth. He is six days old today. My mother was such a big help with our two-year-old. She added a level of comfort so that I could labor. I didn't have another thing to worry about besides giving birth. My husband didn't have to leave my side the whole time. And my mother got to bond with her grandchildren!

> *Mary:* We had a Homefirst nurse at our home birth. She helped me with visualization. I said, 'Talk to me!" during the contractions. She said, "Imagine the baby's eyes, nose, little hands." It really helped!

> *Margaret:* My mother was here to handle coffee and coffee cake for whoever was around. It is so important to have someone there to handle whatever comes up and to be hospitable. And, I didn't miss having another miserable ride to the

hospital in the car. My family and friends were here saying, "We are here. We will take care of you."

Dr. Sue, with Homefirst Health Services: There is a period in transition where every woman feels like saying, "Just give me anything to get me through this." At the hospital drugs are administered at this point if they are requested. It is interesting to me that any woman who has been given painkillers in transition will tell you that the medication didn't seem to do anything to help with the pain. But at home the added support of family and friends gets women through and allows them to have a faster labor and delivery without any unnecessary intervention.

Brenda: Self-confidence is so important. American obstetricians destroy that confidence. They make you feel that no one could have a baby naturally. When I visited Homefirst early in my pregnancy, the staff told me I could have a baby at home, I could do it. That is so important!

Denise, Homefirst nurse: "When I was in labor, just being up and around at home was so much better, talking to neighbors, eating and drinking. I don't know any women who don't want to be up and around in labor. It is easier for the doctors to have you in bed and on your back but not easier for the laboring woman.

Linda: Knowledge of your body and what it is going through was important to me, knowing that the cervix was thinning out with each contraction. Each contraction was getting me closer to delivery and relaxed breathing between the contractions helped so much.

Anna: With our third baby I decided to work with the contractions. I decided to imagine the baby's head coming out of the cervix. I imagined myself opening wider and wider to let the baby out. This baby was born on our water bed and I was so comfortable. Right away I could fall asleep, nurse, rest in my bed — all the things you can't do in the hospital.

Elizabeth, Homefirst nurse: The most important thing is to surrender to what is happening to you during birth, surrender to the birthing energy and let all other aspects out of your mind.

Terry: I believe there are three things that help. Number one, have your husband there. Number two, both husband and wife should have childbirth education; and number three, do some physical preparation. Get your body ready to deliver, prepare for squatting. That is what helped me the most.

Mary Lou: The right medical staff is so important. I knew I wouldn't need an episiotomy because I trusted my medical staff to give me what I wanted. At Homefirst they felt I could do it.

Husbands, come with your wives to prenatal care visits. Your pregnant wife is carrying the treasure of your family. Coming in with her says, "I know you can do it!" The point of confidence cannot be underestimated. The team in sports, to use another sports analogy, which has the most confidence will most often win the game.

I believe every child is a premium child. The only way to bring about healthy premium children is with a lack of interference in the birth process. To use Dr. Tucker's famous words, she would tell all her doctors and nurses, "Your role at the birth is not to deliver the baby. Your role is to be the lifeguard, to employ a watchful expectancy. You make sure that every woman has a comfortable environment. Then if there is a problem, do something."

And that is the home court advantage.

Consumers Are Getting Smarter

One of the doctors on my staff recently said, "I like how consumers are getting smarter! Those consumers who have properly compared the home birth option with hospital offerings are the ones who return as our patients." He is absolutely right.

It is essential that I provide for consumers not only information but also an implementation for home birth. It is not enough to explain the dangers of hospital birth and the safety of home birth. I must help consumers take action on behalf of their families' emotional and physical well-being.

Implementation is what makes this book different from every other birthing book I have read. The reader can come away not only with information on home birth but with a safe birth plan to follow. Homefirst has a birthing system with an implementation and a proven safety record. Those looking for safe birth experiences can have them now. It is not a dream of the future.

Consumers are not condemned to attempting a safe birth by fighting as best they can in the hospital delivery room. The Homefirst birthing system is in place now for any healthy woman, regardless of age, to have a home birth. This is very exciting to me to be a part of this movement in America.

Instruments and Equipment For Home Birth

Initially families explore home birth as consumers. They ask excellent consumer questions about my practice and the implementation of home birth. Families reading this book as consumers might be interested in seeing the following lists of supplies and equipment — items brought to the homes by the medical staff and items provided by families at the time of birth.

The medical staff of Homefirst Health Services brings to the home of the expectant parents the following instruments and emergency equipment, in all over 100 pieces of sophisticated technological equipment. Much of the listed equipment below is brought to the home in sterile and disposable packaging.

In the instrument bag:

1 instrument tray with cover
1 long needle holder
1 short needle holder

2 mosquito forceps
4 straight jaw forceps for clamping cord
3 ring forceps
1 scissors for cutting cord
1 episiotomy scissors
1 vaginal speculum
1 10" allis forceps
2 Jackson retractors
1 pair Simpsons obstetrical forceps
plastic Hollister cord clamps or suitable ligature
    material
suture material: 2-0 and 2-0 chromis
lubricating jelly
sterile examining gloves
sterile gauntlet glove
gauze pads 3" x 3"
16 fr. urethral catheter
Amnihook
Barrier sterile field
enema bag, disposable
sphygomanometer and cuff
fetoscope (Delee-Hillis)
stethoscope
spring scale to weigh baby
bulb syringe (sterile disposable)
Delee suction trap with catheter (sterile disposable)
local anesthetic (nesacaine 2%)
ergotrate tab 0.2 mg.
$AgNO_3$ 1% and saline eye rinse
Uristix (test for protein in urine)

Section One: Homefirst Health Services

Emergency Equipment

normal serum albumin
lactated ringers and normal saline 1000cc.
Y-Type blood infusion tubing set
intravenous angiocaths: 18 and 20 gauge
butterfly infusion sets: 19 and 25 gauge
adhesive tape and bandaids
syringes: 3, 12, 20 cc.
needles: 18, 20, 22, 25 gauge tourniquet
Air shields Ambu Bag — newborn size
anatomical face masks: newborn & premature
  sizes
endotracheal tubes: 2.5, 3.0, and 3.5
bulb syringe
Delee suction trap
Electronic fetal monitor
laryngoscope with #0 and #1 Miller blades
Vacutainer sleeve, needles, and red top blood collection tubes, umbilical artery catheter
newborn feeding tube
injectable Demerol
injectable epinephrine 1/1000
injectable ergotrate, 1.2 mg
injectable and buccal pitocin
injectable saline
injectable $NaHCO_3$
injectable magnesium sulfate
injectable calcium gluconate
ergotrate tablets, 0.2 mg
sterile H_2O

66

portable oxygen
floodlights
bed board

Preparing Your Home For Birth

Families preparing their homes for birth must have the following supplies available for labor and delivery.

In the Bedroom

A. For the bed
1. *Waterproofing: fitted vinyl mattress cover, shower curtain or painter's plastic drop cloth*
2. *Bedrest with arms*
3. *Pillows: 2 large, 2 small, extra throw pillows*

B. For protecting the floor:
Small stack of newspapers, about 6 inches

C. For medical equipment:
A cleared dresser lined with newspapers

D. For delivery
1. *Washcloths — four*
2. *Towels — six large*
3. *Underpads, one box (23 x 36 or 17 x 23)*
4. *Sanitary napkins — one box hospital size and belt*
5. *Flashlight*
6. *Floor lamp — lightweight, portable*

7. *Plastic garbage bags — three large for lining boxes for waste*
8. *Two chairs*
9. *Rocking Chair*
10. *Footstool*
11. *Nightgown easy for nursing baby*
12. *Receiving blanket*
13. *Diapers, clothes for baby*

Optional:t
Crockpot for heating wet towels
Fleet enema
Gauze pads 3x3
Box of disposable diapers
Heating pad
Olive oil
Camera, film
Bowl for placenta

In the Kitchen
A. Drinks
1. *Fruit juices, including one tray frozen juice cubes*
2. *Herbal (noncaffeinated) teas*
3. *Protein drinks to keep up energy*

B. Miscellaneous
1. *Flexible straws*
2. *Pots — three quart and four quart*
3. *Steam kettle for boiling water*
4. *Prepared and frozen meals for week after birth*

Cesarean Section Prevention

"All great truths begin as blasphemies."
— George Bernard Shaw
from Annajansk

"The doctors all told me I was crazy to want to try a (vaginal birth after cesarean) birth," Marie, a caller to my radio show, said on the air.

"I am a nurse working in labor and delivery. I really believe that my first two babies were c-section deliveries because I placed more faith in my doctors than in myself.

With my first baby my water bag broke and there were no contractions. At the hospital they told me to go to bed and stay there. Later that afternoon, even though I was making progress, they scheduled surgery telling me I was a case of 'failure to progress.' I really wish they had let me labor longer. I feel I could have done it myself.

I searched for an obstetrician willing to discuss a birth with my second child. Five doctors all said I should just schedule a c-section birthday for my baby. I can't believe I did as they said, but I couldn't find any support to try for a natural delivery.

The third time I was pregnant I said, 'Never again!' I found a support group which helped me deal with the trauma of c-section surgery and prevent it from happening to me again. They steer you to doctors with low c-section rates and give you all the encouragement and information to try again for a natural delivery.

My third labor last fall was identical to my first one. My water bag broke but this time I stayed home. I walked and walked, drank fluids, talked to neighbors and went to the hospital as late as I could. I refused to get into bed. I pushed for only forty minutes this time and pushed out my largest baby, 8 pounds, 4 ounces.

There is a huge difference in the two styles of delivery. With the c-sections I was uncomfortable for weeks. With natural delivery it's over when it's over. I was so pleased to have finally been permitted to have my baby myself. It is really sad how the doctors told me I couldn't possibly do it the second time. I know now I could have!"

Marie is a very courageous woman. She had such a desire for more children and for natural labor that she was able to defy modern obstetrical practices to get what she wanted. Her story is one of many sad cases of unscientific medical practice that is all too common today. Even the American College of Obstetrics and Gynecology has stated that the cesarean section surgery rate is up in the United States and that rate is too high.

We have reached a time when women have to become educated about cesarean section prevention long before the birth of their first children. In the 1980s unnecessary cesarean sections are analogous to environmental hazards. In order to be protected from radon gas in your home, for example, you must be informed of the dangers and take the appropriate action to protect your family from the hazards. The same is true of c-section surgery. Education is the best prevention method families have from this hazardous surgery.

I use the term hazardous because it is. In 1987 a 14-state survey from the Center for Disease Control indicated that babies over 1500 grams (3.1 pounds) are more likely to die if born by cesarean section than if born vaginally. The risk is many times greater to the mother also when surgery is performed. Recovery from c-section surgery is painful and slow, leaving the mother with psychological, as well as abdominal, scars.

Our goal as doctors must be to deliver healthy babies to healthy mothers. Doctors must aim to make America the safest country in the world in which to have a baby. We now rank 24th among the top 20 industrialized nations for infant and maternal mortality. It is unethical and unthinkable that any doctor would be performing unnecessary c-sections in his or her own best interest, rather than the best interests of the mother and baby. But it is happening with great frequency today.

In the past ten years doctors have been delivering babies by cesarean section at a 6% rate, eight years ago at a 10% rate, five years ago at a 15% rate and three years ago at a 20% rate. In 1987 a jump to between 30 and 35% occurred, translating into one million plus Americans having c-section deliveries in that year. Doctors supposedly have increased their c-section rates in the U.S. as one means of decreasing our infant mortality but the infant mortality rate has risen dramatically.

About one in four women is now having this surgery for the delivery of her child. In Illinois alone in 1987, according to a Chicago Sun Times report of March 16, l988, there was a 10% increase in cesarean sections. Blue Cross/Blue Shield of Illinois is urging hospitals to slow the growing rate of birth by surgery. The National Institutes of Health (N.I.H.), a neutral body, likewise says that there are too many cesareans being performed. N.I.H. believes that obstetricians aren't willing to make a change to improve this statistic.

These findings really hit home for my staff and me when our practice had a booth at a baby fair in Chicago a few years ago. We were at the fair to explain the home birth option to those who didn't know that babies could be born at home. However, over the course of the fair, about 1,000 women who had previously had cesarean section deliveries stopped by our booth to talk.

Many of them were pregnant again and returning to their same obstetricians for planned, repeat c-section deliveries. They were feeling their bodies had failed them and were wondering if surgery would really be necessary the second time. We were shocked and realized we had to do something to help these women.

With the c-section rate rising as it is, before too long all women will be having c-sections, a ridiculous but plausible thought. We felt we had to intervene to change this statistic. Since our own c-section rate was about 4% we felt there must be something we could do to provide safer deliveries for so many women fearing unnecessary repeat surgery for the births of their next infants. Our research led us to some very positive conclusions.

Why So Many C-Sections?

Statistics collected by my staff revealed that 90-92% of all pregnant women should be able to deliver their babies without any medical intervention at all. It was puzzling to me, then, why so many doctors were choosing a measure so drastic as surgery for the delivery of so many babies.

According to the March 16, 1988, *Sun Times* article referred to earlier,

> ". . . doctors in major teaching hospitals tend to have lower c-section rates because doctors there have a heightened awareness of the overuse of c-sections."

This implies that with doctor awareness the rate could be lowered. This article was clearly saying that doctors are the cause of so many c-sections. There has been no significant change in this picture since this 1988 article.

Everyone knows why Blue Cross/Blue Shield is mentioned in the article as being interested in lowering the c-section rate. Theirs is the financial interest of an insurer who has to pay out much more per birth on a c-section delivery. Currently c-sections average about $3,000 more per birth than a natural delivery. Blue Cross/Blue Shield's research was saying the same thing to hospitals — there are too many unnecessary c-sections for which they are having to pay. Dr. Norbert Gleicher, former Director of Maternal-Fetal Medicine at Mount Sinai Medical Center in Chicago, is quoted in the article as being concerned that unnecessary c-sections expose women to risks for infection and other problems. He believes the bottom line is going to have to be financial.

> "Scientific data and education haven't been enough to get doctors to lower the rates. . . . If insurers want to reduce the c-section rate, they will have to give doctors and hospitals a financial incentive for vaginal deliveries."

This certainly implies that doctors are doing c-sections for the added income which this surgery generates.

So here again, in the c-section rate we see more

unscientific medicine being practiced. Doctors are protecting their own interests, whatever they may be. C-
sections provide ego gratification, a false sense of security from lawsuits, additional income, and the false
assumption that they have given their patients a safer
delivery. These are powerful obstacles to hurdle if you
are an uninformed patient. The less the patient knows
about medical science, the greater the chance of a c-section. It has become imperative to be an educated pregnant woman in order to have a safe labor and delivery.

Doctors' Myths About Cesarean Section

The doctors in my practice did further research. The
reasons for most c-sections were not grounded in good
scientific practice but rather in doctor myths such as,
"Once a c-section, always a c-section." A whole body of
medical phrases had been invented to justify falsely the
surgical delivery of infants. Mothers were being told
that: they had "failure to progress" in labor; the baby's
head was too large for the pelvis; they had a "cephalo-
pelvic disproportion"; twins and breech babies must be
delivered by c-section, and that vaginal delivery after a
previous c-section is dangerous due to the likelihood of
"uterine rupture."

These reasons for c-section and repeat c-section
surgery are most of the time unfounded. In 1987, c-section surgery was the number one surgical procedure
being performed in the United States and it still is today
as we enter a new century.

The *New York Times* National edition of Sunday,

Section One: Homefirst Health Services

May 22, 1994 states,

"Each year, some 420,000 deliveries of babies in the United States use unnecessary cesarean sections, a consumer group has contended.

'The highest rates are in the South and at large for-profit hospitals,' the Public Citizen Health Research Group said on Wednesday. But it said that surgical deliveries were dropping slightly and that more women were delivering babies vaginally after previous cesareans."

The group examined birth records that show 22.6 percent of the nearly four million births in 1992 were cesarean, making the operation the most common major surgery performed in this country. That is down slightly from a 22.7 percent cesarean rate in 1991. Cesareans, commonly known as c-sections, often save the lives of babies during long or complicated labor, but the surgery can also endanger the mother. In 1970, cesareans were used in 5.5 percent of births, but they skyrocketed to 24.7 percent in 1988.

Consumer advocates say only 12 percent of births should be by Caesarean, and the Center for Disease Control and Prevention advocates a rate of no higher than 15 percent.

Using the 12 percent mark, the consumer group said, about 420,000 unnecessary c-sections were performed at a cost of $1.3 billion in 1992.

Women are being deprived of delivering their babies for reasons other than those stated to them by doctors.

76

Could doctors actually believe that c-sections are safer and easier than natural delivery? This is absurd. It is impossible to comprehend that an ethical practitioner would choose a procedure "safer" for himself and more dangerous for the mother and her baby. Various studies have indicated that c-section delivery is from eight to 26 times more dangerous than natural delivery. Mothers and babies are suffering unnecessarily, and even dying, from cesarean deliveries today.

A 1986 publication of the Public Citizen Health Research Group entitled "Unnecessary Cesarean Sections: A Rapidly Growing National Epidemic" states that:

"The three most important medical causes contributing to the rapid national increase in c-section rates are:
1. the continued use of the outdated policy of automatic repeat c-section for women who have already had a c-section,
2. the overdiagnosis and overuse of c-section for dystocia (or abnormal labor), and
3. the overdiagnosis of fetal distress."

These three categories contributed to 93.4% of the increase in national c-section rates from 1980 to 1985. These figures have not changed significantly since then.

C-section surgery does have a few benefits for an insecure, fearful or inexperienced doctor. Surgery is quicker than waiting for labor and delivery to happen on its own. It seems safer to the doctor because he or she doesn't have to watch the mother progress through the pains of labor. It is difficult for doctors to watch hospital labor which can be a tremendously lengthy and anxious experience for everyone. Obstetricians who don't understand the scientific principles of labor and delivery might actually think they are saving mothers from a lot of pain by performing a c-section. We know they think they are saving themselves from potential lawsuits.

But these are incorrect and unethical reasons for performing surgery on any pregnant woman. As one of the new doctors on my staff put it, "We were trained in medical school that a pregnant woman is something to be feared. She is considered ill until she delivers and the sooner the better."

Ways to Reduce the C-Section Rate

An article from *Family Practice News Women's Health*, January 1, 1997 outlines a plan for the reduction of the current cesarean section rate based on a collaborative program sponsored by the Institute for Healthcare Improvement (IHI), Boston, a nonprofit organization that aims to improve health care delivery.

"At a meeting on reducing cesarean section rates sponsored by IHI (14 months after the collaborative began,) participants shared information about what worked and what didn't. Dr. Bruce Flamm, who chaired the congress, noted that while both the U.S. Public Health Service and the World Health Organization have set a cesarean section rate target of 15% by the year 2000, not everyone shares that goal. 'If you agree that the current 23% rate should be reduced, there are safe ways to do it,' Dr. Flamm, area research chairman and practicing OB/GYN, at Kaiser Permanente, Riverside, California said.

The following are "change concepts", that organizations in the mulitcenter collaborative were encouraged to follow to reduce unnecessary cesarean sections. "The science is not new, but the framework is," Dr. Flamm said. "The more you do, the better, but you don't have to do everything. Pick one small change you can implement by next Tuesday," he advised.

Avoid Unnecessary Interventions

Interventions such as artificial rupture of membranes or induction often result in imposition of time limits and cesarean section if the baby isn't delivered within that time. Instead, do only what's absolutely necessary and no more.

— *Use expectant management for spontaneous rupture of membranes rather than immediate routine induction.*

— *Do not routinely induce for postdates, prior to 42 weeks gestation, unless there are other indications.*

— *Avoid estimating fetal weight by ultrasound after 36 weeks.*

— *Consider using intermittent monitoring or auscultation instead of routine electronic fetal*

monitoring.
— *Give patients a "due week", rather than a "due date".*

Provide effective labor support

It is important to treat labor as a natural, physiologic process and not to over-rely on technology.
— *Provide one-to-one psychological support through nurses or doulas.*
— *Give oral hydration to assist patients in their physical efforts and reduce the impression that they're being prepared for surgery.*
— *Turn off electronic fetal monitors except at change of shift; have nurses spend more time talking to the patients.*

Manage high-risk conditions

Conditions such as herpes simplex virus, twin pregnancies, and breech presentations should not be seen as automatic indications for cesarean delivery.
— *Develop and use criteria for vaginal delivery in patients with genital herpes.*
— *Develop and use criteria for trial of labor in twin gestations, based on gestational age and fetal positions.*
— *Use external cephalic version at 37 weeks*

gestation for breech presentation.
To avoid unnecessary repeat cesarean sections:
— Plan a trial of labor
— Use American College of Obstetrical and
   Gynecological guidelines and other criteria for
   elective repeat cesarean section and use these
   to develop vaginal birth after cesarean ()
   guidelines. Circulate to all staff.
— Review all repeat cesarean sections to ascer-
   tain medical necessity either as a posthoc
   review process or as precertification.

Exposing the Myths

My staff and I did much investigating of the explanations given to families for their c-section deliveries. We discovered fallacies in all the explanations.

The doctors' myth, "Once a c, always a c," has never been proven. This statement, first made by an intoxicated physician at a medical meeting, is only espoused by doctors with no understanding of the contractility of the uterus. The uterus is a tremendously strong muscle. It contracts as other muscles do in order to function. Much as the heart muscle contracts to pump blood, the uterine muscle contracts and expands in labor to deliver the baby. A scar on the uterus from a previous c-section negligibly lowers its ability to contract properly. So you might say that for most women the opposite of this myth is true, "Once a c section, next time a vaginal birth." Each labor is unique and a doctor is suspect who prejudges the outcome of the next labor after a c-section.

Many women whose obstetricians have scared them with the threat of a repeat c-section ask me how any woman who has had a previous c-section could be a low risk patient in my practice. They have all been labeled by their obstetricians as high risk due to their last deliveries. In reality, provided the woman is in good health, she should be treated no differently from any other pregnant woman. She will become high risk only if doctors use interventionist measures on her at the time of delivery or if there is a new indication.

Another doctors' myth, about which women are so frequently warned, the feared "uterine rupture," occurs rarely in births subsequent to c-sections. Contrary to the doctors' myth, scientific literature supports that the uterus does not rupture from and has not been weakened by a previous c-section delivery. Two investigators reported in separate presentations to the American College of Obstetricians and Gynecologists that they "have been unable to find a single report of a maternal death due to rupture of a low transverse uterine incision in the more than 11,000 trials of labor." This statement was made after reviewing data collected at the University of California, Los Angeles, School of Medicine; Kaiser Permanente Medical Centers; and the University of California, Irvine, School of Medicine (as reported in Family Practice News; Volume 18, No. 14, July 15-31, 1988). Uterine rupture is just another well-propagated myth.

Then there is the often-used expression, "failure to progress," which leads to surgery. Doctors use this phrase at hospital births for several reasons. They have placed women flat on their backs and on the hospital's timetable for delivery. If progress isn't made in a given amount of time, they prepare for surgical delivery. But "failure to progress" is predictable if a woman is on her back for eight or nine hours and pushing in this very unnatural position.

It becomes a different matter if someone, at home, who is walking around and squatting during labor has "failure to progress." The laboring woman has then done everything in her power to deliver in a reasonable amount of time. However, as I have discussed in a previous chapter, timetables for labor get distorted in the hospital. Labor time in the hospital doubles because doctors don't make the best use of that time. Dr. Emanuel Friedman of Boston's Beth Israel Hospital and Harvard Medical School has stated that 70% of cesareans for prolonged labor are unnecessary.

Hand in hand with "failure to progress" goes another classic mythical reason for c-section deliveries -CPD- "cephalo-pelvic disproportion." This first myth leads doctors to suspect the second. "Cephalo-pelvic disproportion" means that the baby's head is too large for delivery through the mother's too small pelvis. It is easy for doctors to incorrectly conclude that if a woman has "failure to progress," it is because the baby's head is too large for delivery. In reality, this doesn't happen very often. Nature allows women to grow babies to a size proper for delivery by that individual mother. If this were really a problem occurring frequently in nature all babies born to small women less than five feet tall would be c-section babies.

Babies born at home to mothers who have had previous c-sections are usually larger than the previous cesarean-born babies. The later, natural born babies disprove the disproportion problem (CPD) by being larger than their older siblings at birth. Generally, it is improperly used labor time or an unwarranted fear of birth accidents which prompts doctors to write CPD on the mother's chart and prepare her for surgery.

The myth that twins and breech babies must be delivered by surgery is a ridiculous notion also. Doctors have been intervening in these types of births for so long that the skills necessary to deliver them have been lost. It actually requires a five-year training program to teach doctors properly to deliver twins and breech babies. However, a new doctor can learn to do a c-section in about 90 days. Preference for the shorter training time has virtually eradicated all knowledge of natural delivery of these babies from U. S. hospitals.

The Birth of HBAC

In the past, my staff and I had assisted women in hospitals who were trying to have vaginal births after cesareans. We noticed that they succeeded only about 50 to 60% of the time in the hospital. We felt sure that it was due to the foreign environment and its interventions. We felt that a higher success rate could be achieved at home for the same reasons that any other woman has an easier time delivering at home. It seemed unnecessary to hospitalize these women at all if the literature were correct. All reputable obstetrical literature states that these women are no different from anyone else in labor if they have no other medical complications.

So a plan evolved within my practice, in the summer of 1987, to let women labor, at home, in the comfort of their own surroundings, with the support of their families, and the careful monitoring of our medical staff. This project became known as Home Birth After Cesarean (HBAC).

We chuckle to ourselves when we look back to those first births. In the name of safety two doctors and two nurses from the practice were sent to these HBAC women's homes. Of course it soon became apparent, due to careful prenatal screening, there was no need for more medical support than at any other home birth. Eighty-seven percent of women in this pilot group had their babies at home with no complications or need for intervention.

This program was a tremendous success. So successful that, now, potential HBAC mothers attend our childbirth classes alongside those who have had successful home births in the past. There is no reason to treat these women differently from other pregnant women.

We do have a few additional recommendations for HBAC mothers. We tell them not to return to the doctor who performed the first c-section surgery. That doctor will view the returning woman as someone with a medical problem. That doctor will, chances are, have his or her mind made up in advance that there will be complications.

We also suggest that couples connect with a Vaginal Birth After Cesarean (VBAC) support group. Jane, leader of a Support Group in Chicago says, "If women attend our sessions, they increase their chances of having a vaginal birth. We help them lay to rest the fear of uterine rupture and try to connect them with doctors who will give them a fair chance at a vaginal delivery. C-section mothers have been stripped of all confidence in their bodies' ability to give birth and they need the support of other women who have been there to regain their confidence. It is a lack of education and the feeling that the doctor is always right that leads to many c-sections. This is what we work on. Being at home for the next birth and knowing how to give birth helps so much!"

How To Prevent a First, Second or Tenth C-Section

Kim, a Homefirst nurse, says she always asks first-time moms, planning to have their babies in the hospital, how they plan to beat the odds of having a c-section. It is getting harder every day to beat the odds with one in four deliveries being a surgical one. Kim asks the expectant moms what chances they personally would like to have for a natural delivery. Kim tells them the mother's chances are diminished greatly by the very act of walking into a hospital.

If someone were to ask me how they could best prepare themselves for a natural delivery and how to avoid a c-section delivery, I'd tell them to first find a doctor with a positive attitude about birth and families. Women should not hesitate to interview doctors before placing themselves in their care. They should be asking the doctors about their c-section rates, about their use of drugs, episiotomies and forceps at delivery.

If a woman has had a previous c-section, she should ask what her chances are of having another one. If the answer sounds like a c-section is very likely, she should run as fast as she can out of his office and look for a more positive practitioner. Once a woman is in labor it is too late to try fighting with an unscientific doctor who has no intention of changing his delivery style for her benefit.

If American women want to help lower the c-section rate in the United States, then they have to start telling their doctors how they feel. Women must tell doctors who are using interventionist methods in a large number of cases that they know he or she hasn't been reading and following current medical literature. They have to say that if the doctors aren't following current recommendations on these matters then they will have to choose other physicians for the births of their babies.

Next I'd tell expectant parents not to take childbirth classes affiliated with a hospital. The childbirth instructors weave topics into their classes which they are forced to include by the hospital staff. For example, Lamaze class instructors spend some time discussing the drugs you will be given in labor. If this is the philosophy of the doctors on staff at any particular hospital then drugs in labor become standard practice for all laboring women.

And, as I said earlier, I tell expectant parents to attend a support group if they have had a previous c-section delivery. These groups provide emotional support and childbirth education to parents of babies born by cesarean section. I like the idea of support. It is similar in style to La Leche League, in that women who have been through the experience of cesarean section are there to support and answer questions of those who are emotionally and physically recovering from c-sections.

One of my callers, on the radio show, commented that she didn't want any other children after having every medical intervention possible with her c-section delivery. But after she went to a VBAC Support Group she decided to have another baby and did have a successful home birth four years after the birth of her first child. "Lots of women don't know that there is help out there. They feel the doctor is always right," she said.

Jane, a VBAC leader familiar with my practice, says that attending VBAC group meetings does increase the couple's chances of having a natural delivery. "Even if there are complications and another c-section is needed next time, the couple's attitude is much better for having had the support of the group," Jane tells VBAC couples.

VBAC literature also tells couples not to return to the same doctor who did the first c-section. Chances are excellent that he or she will be prejudging the VBAC woman based on her first delivery.

I have seen so many times in my fifteen years of practice that labor and delivery can vary immensely from a first delivery to a second or third or tenth. There is seldom a reason to predict a woman's next labor pattern based or her last delivery. But doctors do try to make these predictions and some will even say that another c-section is inevitable. For this reason, if at all possible, women should get the second opinion of a home birth doctor long before delivery.

It should give hope to women, who are fearing a repeat of their first c-section experience, to know that labor can come in infinite varieties for any given woman. I have seen births subsequent to a c-section take place with no problems, only thirty minutes of pushing, and the safe delivery of a baby much larger than the older sibling.

Our current success rate is 90% . We at Homefirst have delivered over 1,000 HBAC babies through 1999. So why take the advice of a doctor who recommends or suspects a second c-section to be necessary? These doctors are placing 90% of women who can have a natural delivery in a very dangerous category — with the other 10% who really need high tech intervention to deliver their babies.

We recommend increasing your chances of having a smooth delivery by having a woman coach. We have noticed that the best coaches for labor are women who have had children of their own and, ideally, the laboring woman's own mother. This is not to say that husbands have no role in labor. In fact, they have a very important role, but they should not be the only ones timing contractions and coaching their wives. It seems that women most want their husbands' presence in the room. They need the unique support husbands have to give. And, ideally, laboring women also can have the support of another woman who knows how labor feels and how to make another woman comfortable during this time.

One mother explained it so well when she called in to The Homefirst Family Health Forum radio show. Sally said, "During my second pregnancy I met a woman in the library who had just had a home birth. I was telling her about the difficult time I had had with my first c-section delivery. We became friends and she came to the home birth of our second child. I really wanted her there. I needed that calm, confident energy. She had been through it. I had only five hours of labor at home. I feel very healed for having had a home birth."

I also tell expectant mothers they can increase their confidence, knowledge and potential for an easy birth by attending La Leche League meetings before the baby is born. We suggest that all pregnant patients attend. There is nothing like the support of other mothers at such a special time. Too many people view the League as being there if a problem arises. However, in a more positive vein, it is important to see mothers who have successfully nursed their babies and to hear information on birth, nursing, nutrition and child care. It is a tremendous confidence-builder for a new mother to know a whole group of women she can get in touch with when she has questions or problems.

There are no doctors who know as much about nursing as the women in La Leche League. In our culture, where there is so much disapproval of nursing and so much misinformation about it, La Leche League, in a sense, gives mothers permission to nurse their babies successfully. La Leche League actually takes the place of grandmothers in many families. Grandmothers used to live nearby or with the expectant family. They would pass on to their daughters and granddaughters all they knew about nursing. Today those who attend League meetings will find the nursing support once present within the family network. Mothers are more likely to have a successful nursing experience if they attend meetings. You can't lose with this support system.

And, of course, women who choose home birth have the best chance of natural delivery. Any woman doing research into safe alternatives will find no more scientific or safe way to deliver than home birth. The concept of will soon become as obvious as home birth. Home birth lowers the amount of labor time and increases the probability of a healthy baby and mother over a routine scheduled c-section.

Birthdays are joyful events. Birth is a happy occasion. And there is no happier birthing situation than being in your own bed, surrounded by loving family and friends. There are no faster births than home births and no better healing opportunities for those who have had hospital deliveries or c-sections than a subsequent home birth. I hope the studies of my practice can result in many more women having happy birth day parties for their infants born safely at home.

Breastfeeding

*"Breasts are more skillful at compounding
a feeding mixture
than the hemisphere of
the most learned professor's brain."*
— *Oliver Wendell Holmes, M.D.*

Dr. Sue, one of the Homefirst Health Services physicians, related a personal story to my radio audience. When she was a new mother, she was determined to nurse her daughter. "Nursing just had to work for me," she said on the air, "because everything else about Erica's hospital birth was so disappointing. We had planned for a natural delivery but in the hospital had one unnecessary intervention after another. The natural experience of nursing became very important to me after our unnatural birth experience.

"My doctor told me to wash my breasts with sterile water before and after each feeding. In no time this advice created a disaster. I developed a terrible rash on both breasts. I was very uncomfortable and nursing Erica was quite painful. My breasts were cracked, bleeding and itchy. When I could no longer stand it, I sought the advice of another doctor who told me to stop washing my breasts. I had developed eczema from the constant irritation of the sterile water."

The doctor shares her unfortunate story to show the disastrous effects of incorrect nursing information. "Even though I was a doctor myself, my nursing information was limited to a few lectures in medical school. Doctors just don't learn much about it. So I didn't know that there is no need for special washing before or after nursing.

"All women should go to La Leche League even before their babies are born," she recommends. "This will increase, tremendously, their ability to nurse and to enjoy nursing their babies. Doctors are complicating, and even terminating nursing, for many mothers and babies, based on doctor myths about breastfeeding. There is no better source of support and information than La Leche League."

Nursing Means Superior Health

I only semi-jokingly have said that this chapter should be one sentence long. One of my staff nurses came to the same conclusion. Our one sentence chapter would read, "Just do it!"

Breastfeeding a baby is as simple a concept as home birth, in some ways. It gives infants the best start in life and maintains optimum health.

I was taught in medical school that breast and bottle feeding were about the same. But during the fifteen years I have been in practice, study after study has consistently shown that nutritionally, psychologically, and medically, nursing is superior to bottle feeding.

In my practice I see virtually 100% nursing infants because I so highly endorse it to home birth families. Over the years we have had over 100,000 pediatric visits to the office and the majority of these are well baby visits. Very few infants have been seen for allergies, eczema, asthma, ear infections, bronchitis or pneumonia. The nursing of babies dramatically improves their health, decreasing the probability of them having these problems.

I have seen two or three cases of asthma over the years. It just rarely happens in the breast-fed baby. Consequently, my patients have fewer office visits with their infants.

You Can't Fool Mother Nature!

I will continue to promote nursing because it is right. Mother nature is the supreme healer and provider of superior nutrition for infants. There will never be a formula that can substitute for mother's milk. There will never be a relationship so important to our children's development as the nursing relationship they have from birth with their mothers.

This relationship is explained so well in an address by Dr. Herbert Ratner on "The Natural Institution of the Family", in 1987. He said to the tenth convention of the

Section One: Homefirst Health Services

Fellowship of Catholic Scholars,

> "Jesus, for instance, tells us to love our neighbor. But Jesus does not instruct the mother how to love her closest and dearest neighbor, the newborn. Thus the mother is not told to nurse or breastfeed her baby. [Jesus] assumes that with eyes to see, with the milk dripping from postpartum breasts, with hungry suckling lips rooting in search of the mother's teats, the woman can figure this out for herself."

No matter how much knowledge a mother has, no matter how much education, the mother who accepts nature, not the doctor, as possessing Wisdom, need not know the reason, but she remains ahead of science.

Artificial feeding is an attempt to fool nature, but the bottom line is that it can't happen. Our society is paying heavily with the health and very lives of our children, by providing an inferior imitation of nature's nutritional plan. Breast milk is a precious natural resource that we in our society are all too willing to waste. It is every bit as essential to our children's growth as adequate rainfall is to the growth of our farmers' crops.

The late Dr. Robert Mendelsohn said that it is imperative for physicians to demand that mothers nurse. Bottle feeding places the health and welfare of infants in our society at risk. There is certainly truth in his words. Every year in the United States there are around 4 million infants born. They are born into a society which doesn't promote nursing and many of them die of complications from the inferior substitutes they are fed. The United States has the highest infant mortality rate among the top twenty industrialized nations. The use of infant formula has helped to place us in the last position and will help to keep us there if its use continues.

Scientists have been trying for over forty years to reproduce breast milk and they have not been successful. Every mother produces milk which is unique for her baby and its needs. It has been discovered that mothers of premature infants produce milk higher in caloric content than that produced for full-term infants. It is nature's way of helping the very small infants gain weight faster, thereby attempting to make up for their prematurity.

The great doctor, Oliver Wendell Holmes, once said, "Breasts are more skillful at compounding a feeding mixture than the hemisphere of the most learned professor's brain." This has certainly proven to be true. Over 100 different components in breast milk have been isolated so far, with an additional one or two being discovered each year.

Formula is no magic concoction. Anyone who reads the ingredients on a can of infant formula will see that it is simply a variation of cow's milk. This is not a safe concoction for infants.

The November 1986 issue of *Parents* magazine tells us that:

" 'Before an infant is a year old, and possibly up

to eighteen months, the kidney is not mature enough to excrete excess amounts of protein as an adult's does,' explains Myron Winick, M.D., director of the Institute of Human Nutrition at Columbia University's College of Physicians and Surgeons. Whole milk contains three times the amount of protein that is in breast milk, which is three times too much. A mother, by depending on whole milk for roughly 50% of her infant's caloric intake, may risk damaging her baby's kidneys."

And from *Baby Talk*, September, 1986:

"Don't drink your milk! The committee on nutrition of the American Academy of Pediatrics recommends that
' . . straight cow's milk is very low in iron. This, plus the iron loss from the minute amount of intestinal bleeding which may be caused by subtle milk allergy, may result in anemia (low iron level in baby's blood) if he or she is switched to regular homogenized milk before one year of age. Cow's milk protein is allergenic to many babies in subtle ways that may not be apparent to parents.' "

As we read further this same article touches on a very contemporary concern of modern parents, obesity in their children. It seems mother nature even has answers for this concern:

"New research has shown that obesity is less of a concern in the breast-fed baby. There are two reasons for this: when breastfeeding, a baby gets different amounts of calories in the milk according to the way he sucks to satisfy different needs. When hungry, a baby sucks vigorously and obtains the higher caloric 'hind milk.' When he is merely thirsty, a baby feeds differently and obtains the thinner, lower caloric 'fore milk.' Also, at about six months, the fat content of breast milk automatically lessens because babies need fewer calories per pound of body weight. For these reasons, 'wanting to nurse all the time' is less likely to cause obesity in a breast-fed baby than in a baby who is fed artificial formula. What a beautiful design nature has!"

Other serious health and economic hazards of cow's milk labeled as formula are demonstrated in the following scientific articles:

Increased infections
Ear infections
"Significantly increased risk for acute otitis media as well as prolonged duration of middle ear effusion were associated with male gender, sibling history of ear infection and not being breast-fed."
— Teele, D.W., "Epidemiology of Otitis Media During the First Seven Years of Life in Greater

Boston: A Prospective Cohort Study."
Journal of Infectious Diseases, 1989
Diarrhea
"Children less than 12 months of age had a lower incidence of acute diarrheal disease during the months they were being breast-fed than children who were fed with formula during the same period." Lerman, Y. et al. "Epidemiology of acute diarrheal diseases in children in a high standard of living settlement in Israel."
— *Pediatric Infectious Disease Journal* 1994; 13(2); 116-22

Respiratory Viral Infections (RSV)
"Breast-feeding was associated with a lower incidence of RSV infection during the first year of life." Holberg, C.J., "Risk Factors for RSV Associated Lower Respiratory Illnesses in the First Year of Life."
— *American Journal Epidemiology*, 1991:133 (135-51)

Increased Incidence of Diseases:
Wheezing
"Breastfeeding seems to protect against wheezing and respiratory tract illnesses in the first four months of life, particularly when other risk factors are present."
Wright, A.L., "Breastfeeding and Lower Respiratory Tract Illnesses in the First Year of Life".

Sudden Infant Death Syndrome (SIDS)
"Not breast-feeding at discharge from an obstetric hospital at any stage of the infant's life was associated with an increased risk of SIDS."
— Mitchell, A. "Results From the First Year of The New Zealand Count Death Study." *New Zealand Medical Association*, 1991; 104:71-76.

Multiple Sclerosis
"Although thought to be multi factorial in origin, and without a clearly defined etiology, lack of breast-feeding does appear to be associated with an increased incidence of multiple sclerosis."
— Dick, G., "The Etiology of Multiple Sclerosis". *Procta Royal Society of Medicine*, 1976;69:611-5

Eczema
"Eczema was less common and milder in babies who were breast-fed (22%) and whose mothers were on a restricted diet (48%). Infants fed casein hydrolyzed, soymilk or cow's milk, 21%, 63% and 70% respectively, developed atopic eczema."
— Chandra R.K., "Influence of Maternal Diet During Lactation and the Use of Formula Feed and Development of Atopic Eczema in the High Risk Infants." *British Medical Journal*, 1989

Insulin Dependent Juvenile Diabetes
"Cow's milk has been implicated as a possible trigger of the auto immune response that destroys pancreatic beta cells in genetically susceptible hosts thus causing diabetes mellitus."
— Karjalainen, et al., *New England Journal of Medicine*, July 30, 1992

Crohn's Disease
"In this study lack of breast-feeding was a risk factor associated with later development of Crohn's Disease in Childhood."
— *British Medical Journal*, 1989

Hodgkin's Disease
"A statistically significant protective effect against Hodgkin's disease among children who are breast-fed at least 8 months compared with children who were breast-fed no more than 2 months."
— Schwartzbaum, J. "An Exploratory Study of Environmental and Medical Factors Potentially Related to Childhood Cancer."
Medical & Pediatric Oncology, 1991; 19(2): 115-21

Delayed Development and Lower Intelligence
Lower IQs
"Children who had consumed mother's milk in the early weeks of life had a significantly higher IQ at 7.5 to 8 years, than those who received no

maternal milk, even after adjustment for differences between groups and mothers' educational and social class."
— Lucas A., "Breast Milk and Subsequent Intelligence Quotient in Children Born Preterm." *Lancet* 1992;339:261-62

"Breast-fed babies have slightly higher IQ's than their cow's-milk-fed peers. The cow does not need to have a better brain."
Lendon Smith, M.D. *Let's Live*, 1997

Financial Savings to Government and Families
One pre-publication study by the Wisconsin State Breast-feeding Coalition estimated the following health care savings in Wisconsin if breast-feeding rates were at 75% at discharge from the hospital and at 50% six months later:
— *$4,645,250/year Acute Otitis Media*
— *$437,120/year Bronchitis*
— *$6,699,600/year Gastroenteritis*
— *$262,440/year Allergies*
— *$758,934 Asthma*
— *$578,500/year Type 1 Diabetes (birth-18 years)*
— *$17,070,000 Breast Cancer*
— *$30,984,432/year TOTAL HEALTH COST SAVINGS*

The $31 million dollar total health cost saving from breastfeeding would translate into 1.5 billion dollars in heath cost savings for the entire United States of America.

Advice From the Experts

This chapter is so important that I have decided to borrow most of what I have to say about nursing from the mouths of the experts, successful nursing mothers and La Leche League leaders themselves.

These women have become the new bearers of information in our culture since there aren't always grandmothers who nursed their children near by to share nursing information. La Leche League members are part of a great support network which can make the difference between a society of healthy or ill children. I cannot stress enough to pregnant women the importance of attending League meetings or making sure they have a personal support team available to get them through those times in infancy that require the calm, experienced advice of other nursing mothers. There are few mothers attending La Leche League meetings who fail at nursing.

All mothers and expectant mothers are welcome at La Leche League International, Inc. meetings. In order to locate the League group meeting nearest your home, you may call their information number in Schaumburg, Illinois, 847-519-7730 or fax 847-519-0035.

And so I continue my chapter with the messages of nursing mothers.

From My Wife, Karen

My dear wife, Karen, has successfully nursed our six children and was a La Leche League leader for many years. She wanted me to be sure to discuss "nursing" in this chapter rather than "breastfeeding." She explains that they are really very different concepts. "Especially in this culture, the nursing mother is often criticized early on by friends and family for overfeeding the baby," she says. "Even strangers will comment to the new mother, 'You just fed that baby. He can't be hungry again!'

"However, there is a lot more going on in nursing than simply nutrition. Babies nurse for a variety of reasons and only one of them is to consume milk.

"There is an exchange between nursing mothers and their babies that no one completely understands or can explain. To the outsider the mother is "overfeeding" her baby but to the baby the mother is comforting him, warming him and communicating with him in ways only he understands. Nursing is really providing nourishment for the physical, psychological, and spiritual needs of the baby."

Karen asks that new mothers not give up during the first few weeks of nursing. "It is like transition in labor. If you can make it over the hump of transition, then you will see your baby. If you can make it through the first few weeks of nursing when you and the baby are adjusting to one another and developing a nursing pattern, then you have made it. You will become a successful and comfortable nursing mother if you get established in the first weeks."

From Laurie

Another successful nursing mother and League member, Laurie, has worked part-time in my office for many years. Her children are older now, and as she looks back, she recommends, "In the early weeks, if the baby is fussy or not gaining weight, do not start giving bottles. This is what doctors tell you to do and it is incorrect information. Babies gain weight on their own timetable first of all. And often when mothers switch over to bottle milk, the fussiness continues or even increases. New mothers must surround themselves with support and 'stick it out.'

"Often these days it is mothers and mothers-in-law who unknowingly undermine the nursing relationship. They frequently tell daughters that nursing didn't work for them either. This erodes the already nervous mother's confidence. Husbands can step in at this point and help considerably. They can be so helpful in the early days of nursing to keep up their wives' confidence. Feeling that you can do it is a large part of success."

Laurie continues, "You have to really want to nurse in order for it to work successfully. Nursing mothers most of the time feel overwhelmed with love for their infants when nursing them. If a tired, nervous mother is trying to nurse and has no support, of course, she won't be feeling this tremendous love. She will feel resentful and will look for permission to stop. This support is essential or the first time someone suggests bottle feeding, the mother will consider it the best option."

From Diane

One mother of two who nursed each child for about six months said, "Please tell nursing mothers to nurse as long as the babies are interested. I so often regret that I stopped too soon. I terminated such beautiful nursing relationships with my children because I was feeling tied down. Little did I know then that by stopping nursing I would be making my job as a mother so much harder. When you stop nursing, you spend much more time trying to compensate for the loss than you spent nursing.

"Our daughter had to be danced to sleep in my arms when I could have been lying down nursing her. My son wouldn't nap without a very lengthy rocking and reading period. What I once thought was tying me down was actually the most efficient and loving thing I could have been doing for all of us. Next time I'll know better."

Advice from La Leche League

Often new mothers hear from their friends and relatives that nursing only worked for them for a week or two. These comments from respected members of the new mother's support network can quickly undermine her confidence. Comments such as, "I lost my milk after a few weeks," seem mysterious, but believable, to an inexperienced nursing mother. She may not know how you simply "lose your milk," but you can be sure that she will begin to wonder when this will happen to her or even worry if her baby's every cry is from hunger.

One of La Leche League's articles, reprinted below, is invaluable in helping the new mother maintain her milk supply. Breast milk doesn't simply disappear after a few weeks as many friends and relatives would have you believe. There is fortunately much known about how to maintain an adequate supply of milk. The following guidelines are sure to make sense of things for any new mother.

Losing Your Milk?

Based on an article by Jayne Polliard, Colorado Springs, Colorado, in the Colorado/Wyoming Insert of LLL News, July/August 1969:

"I don't have enough milk!" "I am drying up!" "My baby isn't gaining enough!" . . . It is NOT time to reach for the formula, nor is it time to wean. It IS time to ask yourself these questions:
1. Are you GIVING BOTH BREASTS AT EACH FEEDING? It isn't logical to stop after only one breast, when your baby is obviously not full and you have a second breast full of milk to give.
2. Are you FEEDING YOUR BABY AS OFTEN AS HE DEMANDS TO BE FED? Adults don't always eat strictly by the clock. They sometimes want to eat a little sooner, depending on how much they ate last time. No one stands guard at the refrigerator to see they don't eat anything before the

appointed time.

3. Are you LETTING YOUR BABY NURSE CONTENTEDLY AS LONG AS HE SEEMS INTERESTED, allowing him to pause and rest, without watching the clock? You don't remove your husband's dinner from the table after an allotted time whether he has finished or not!

4. Are you DRINKING PLENTY OF LIQUIDS in order to replace what is used in making milk, as well as to supply your own needs? Nursing mothers need lots of water either "straight" or in the form of fruit and vegetable juices, milk, or soup. If your urine is dark or orange or small in amount, you are not drinking all you need. (If you get constipated, drink a lot more, especially fruit juices.)

5. Are you EATING WELL? Nursing mothers need good nutritious foods. If you have a small appetite, eat small amounts, but eat often. Don't try to satisfy your hunger with sweets (candy, cookies, cake, pie, etc.) since these will cut down on your appetite for nutritious foods like meat, fish, cheese, eggs, fresh fruits and vegetables. What is best for you is ultimately best for your baby.

6. Do you UNDERSTAND "SUPPLY AND DEMAND"? It means that the more milk your baby takes from you, the more your body will make. Therefore, the more formula you give today, the less milk your body will make tomorrow. Formula supplements are the means to

DECREASE your supply, not increase it.

7. Is your BABY GETTING SOLIDS TOO SOON? Studies have shown that solids also interfere with a previously ample milk supply, and that for normal full-term babies it is best not to introduce them until about the middle of the first year after birth. If for some reason your baby had to have solids earlier, be sure to nurse well on both breasts before offering the solids.

8. Do you know that BABIES HAVE "FREQUEN-CY" DAYS when they nurse more often than usual to bring in more milk for their expanding needs? Denying the baby additional nursing interferes with his efforts to obtain milk according to his growing demands. Remember, appetite parallels growth.

9. Are you COMPARING YOUR BREAST-FED BABY WITH THE BOTTLE-FED BABY? Their daily eating schedule will be dissimilar because breast milk digests more quickly, so nursing babies are hungry sooner. Also, nursing is harder work than the bottle, so the baby tires more quickly and may take less per feeding. This is especially true of premature babies and those under six pounds.

10. Are you TAKING BIRTH CONTROL PILLS? The Food and Drug Administration has warned that they are not to be taken by breastfeeding mothers. They may reduce the supply of her milk as well as have other harmful effects on the milk and on the baby.

11. Are you GETTING ENOUGH REST AND RELAXATION? Fatigue and tension work against good let-down and ample milk supply. New mothers often don't get as much sleep as they need, and this is one reason why feeding time is such a boon for you as well as for your baby. Don't try to do anything else, or even think about anything else, while you are nursing the baby. Get your feet up, relax, and enjoy him. Look at him. Cuddle him. Lie down or sit in a rocker, whatever is easy and comfortable. You might like to arrange for soft music, or a pleasant view — anything to shift the cares of the day from your mind for a while. Baby won't mind if you snooze a bit — he'll let you know if he needs attention, but after he's had his meal he's more likely to drop off to sleep himself in this lovely relaxed atmosphere.

After considering these questions carefully, and taking to heart the ones that seem to apply to you, you should find that your confident attitude and improved nursing how-to will have a remarkable effect on your milk production in a short time — a day or two, or maybe three. So relax and enjoy your baby.

From My Radio Show Call-ins

Many callers to my Saturday Homefirst Family Health Forum radio program have expressed single beneficial ideas about nursing. Experienced mothers always

phrase things better than a doctor ever could so I'd like
to share their exact comments with my readers.

Linda: The percent of women who successfully
nurse after attending a La Leche League series
of meetings is virtually 100%. There is a warm
feeling that surrounds you at the meetings. You
soon forget the difficulties and can enjoy the victory of nursing.

Carol: You need to get out and get support to see
that other people are nursing also. Even though
I later became a League leader, at the time of my
first baby I didn't go to meetings. So when the
baby was six months old, I stopped nursing her.
I interpreted her desire to look around while
nursing as lack of interest. I'm sorry I stopped
because she developed a medical problem
requiring medication which could have been
avoided by nursing. I just didn't have good
information.

Beth: My doctor told me I was too flat-chested to
nurse. He recommended that I not even try it.
But I did go against his advice and nursed my
daughter for 21 months. It was hard at first, not
because I was flat-chested, but because she was
colicky. Luckily my sister was a nursing mom
and a League leader who encouraged me long
distance over the phone.

It is so easy for people to say, "You're
starving your baby; that is why she cries so
much!" when really there is no nursing problem
and the crying would happen regardless of the

feeding method used. As far as breast size, that doctor was all wrong. Milk is stored behind the breast and size has nothing to do with a woman's ability to nurse. Every woman can nurse her baby successfully.

Aggie: My new baby is able to nurse even with a cleft palate. She was born at home last week and has already gained 3 ounces over her birth weight. It was difficult for her to nurse at first because of the separation in the top of her mouth. It was not easy for her to get a good suction.

But last night a woman whom I've never met talked to me over the phone for an hour and a half about how to nurse a cleft palate infant. She was from La Leche League and had nursed her own cleft palate baby fourteen years ago when it seemed to her that no one knew how to do it. It takes a desire to nurse, but it can be done even under exceptional circumstances such as mine.

Jerri: Just keep wanting to nurse your baby and you can do it.

Karen: I'd like to talk about the little-known advantages of nursing.

Mothers and babies are locked in the same R.E.M. sleep patterns at first. New mothers often notice that they wake up during the night slightly before the baby. All the mother has to do is prepare to nurse the baby in bed and both can go back to sleep quickly. It is so subtle that often in the morning husbands think the baby slept through the night.

Another advantage is that nursing from opposite breasts gives the baby equal muscle development on both sides of the body. This eliminates crossed eyes and develops the extremities equally.

Since breasts cannot be propped up somewhere, babies receive the holding they need from their mothers while nursing.

And the fascinating list goes on! Nursing eliminates most allergies in babies. It has been shown to lower the incidence of pre- and post-menopausal cancer in women who have nursed infants for a total of 36 months or more. There is even an economic incentive: you save enough money in six months of nursing to buy a major appliance!

Jo: Don't go to a doctor with your nursing questions. They don't know about nursing and will readily recommend bottle feeding to anyone who finds any problems with nursing. Talk to nursing mothers. Go to La Leche League meetings.

Jean: Women who come to La Leche League after their babies are born generally come because of a problem. Problems seem to develop soon after the infants go to the first pediatric visit because their mothers have collected all kinds of wrong information from their pediatricians.

They come to League having been told about the need for supplemental bottles, keeping the babies out of their beds at all times and other myths promoted by pediatricians.

However, if women come to League meetings while still pregnant, they don't develop unusual problems later in the nursing relationship with their babies.

Dr. Mike, a Homefirst doctor: Families can't afford to entrust the care of their infants to pediatricians these days. They are physicians who work best with children who have unusual diseases and problems. You must choose a doctor who will support the family as a unit, a doctor who advocates nursing and natural childbirth. These doctors are the ones who keep families together and make giving birth to children a joy.

Those families who choose to nurse their infants are participants in one of life's greatest relationships. It is an experience no child or mother should miss. Not every mother may be able to have a home birth, but every mother can nurse her baby. I have often said that if a mother had to choose between having a home birth and nursing her baby, I would persuade her to choose nursing her baby. That is how important it is.

A Summary

*Reality can destroy the dream, why shouldn't the
dream destroy reality?*
— *George Moore*

*T*o one of my Sunday night seminars on home
birth I invited a nurse I had known while
working at Cook County. I had delivered one of
her children at home a few weeks earlier and she was
now attending my seminar with her family to share their
home birth experience. The mother and father spoke
about what a memorable and wonderful event it had
been. Then their teenage children likewise exclaimed
that it was wonderful. Finally their four year old spoke.
He said, "It was nice. I'm going to remember it for about
a day."

The audience roared with laugher.

But when I thought about his choice of words I realized he certainly had the right perspective on birth. To
say he was going to remember it for about a day was to

say that it was a normal kind of occurrence. He didn't see how anyone should be making that big a commotion over something that had been such a normal and natural event in his house.

As in many other instances it takes adults to give the normal and natural course of things all sorts of mystique and complicated procedures. Especially at hospital births these days, all sorts of complex paraphernalia is required for birth: gloves, masks, stirrups, IV's, labor rooms, delivery rooms, recovery rooms etc. A lot of unnecessary medical ritualizing goes on. It is such a prevalent system that most adults accept this ritualizing as necessary for birth. It took a four year old boy to put things in perspective for me and my Sunday night seminar audience.

The Emperor's New Clothes

Of course the little boy's comment at my seminar reminds me of another little boy and another story. Bear with me, it is a related story. And it would be most appropriate for me to conclude my book in my favorite style — digressing.

Birth in America reminds me of the Hans Christian Anderson tale, The Emperor's New Clothes. In this classic tale, two thieves were given a large sum of money to weave clothes for the Emperor. The thieves told the Emperor that anyone who said he could not see the clothes was unfit for the job he did. The two were pocketing the Emperor's money and making royal robes which all the members of his court said were quite beautiful. The Emperor himself was unable to see the robes but couldn't admit this to anyone. He gave the thieves the title of Imperial Court Weavers and decided to wear his new clothes in a grand procession.

When the Emperor walked in the procession all the people standing in the streets said, "How beautiful are the Emperor's new clothes! No one in the crowd would say that he could see nothing, for that would have meant that he was not fit for his job.

It was a child along the procession route who said loudly, "But he has on no clothes!"

Word spread quickly from person to person that the child saw no clothes on the emperor.

Then all at once all the people said, "But he has on no clothes!" The Emperor knew that they were right but he thought to himself, "I must march on. I can't turn back now." His servants marched on behind him holding on to his invisible train which, of course, did not exist at all.

In both stories the children's honest assessments cut through the layers of deception which only adults can create in the first place. Deceptions surrounding birth in this country are so firmly implanted that we can only laugh uncomfortably when a child catches us off guard and reminds us that we have been viewing the Emperor's new clothes from the procession route.

Hope for the Future of America's Birthing System

In sports as in the scientific birth system, one should always assume that the opposing team knows more than your team. In sports this assumption keeps the team players on their toes. In scientific birth it gives you the ultimate hope for a healthier birthing system in the future. There is hope because obstetricians really do know that home birth works best. It has been proven over and over in obstetrical literature that intervention in the birth process and electronic monitoring are generally harmful to healthy women in labor. The Chicago Maternity Center's statistics are overwhelmingly in favor of home birth. Those developed countries having a safe birthing record, such as Sweden, have large home birth components. My own twenty-five years of home birth practice and the years spent by my predecessors are powerful evidence of the safety of home birth when practiced by properly trained scientists. All these facts and figures are hard to ignore.

Obstetricians have this information in their hands but currently the medical establishment is operating in its own best interest. Influential hospital obstetricians have donned the Emperor's new clothes and can not admit that they see the sham of their practices. They are unable to follow the recommendations of their own professional organization, the American College of Obstetricians and Gynecologists, which has called for a reduction in the number of cesarean section deliveries and in the use of electronic fetal monitors. To change their ways is to admit that the field of obstetrics is a dinosaur. It is not relevant to the healthy pregnant woman. Much like the Emperor, obstetricians know what is right but continue to march in the procession.

But there is hope for a new American birthing system. For several reasons the trend simply has to shift. Insurance companies are investigating how fewer health care dollars can be spent in the areas of pregnancy and delivery. Pouring money into extensive prenatal testing, fetal monitoring and interventionist birthing practices such as cesarean section deliveries has not decreased, but has in fact increased, our infant and maternal mortality rates.

Insurance companies have found the American obstetrical system to be unsafe and are working to find a safe alternative. Obstetricians are injuring and even killing mothers and babies and doing so at a very high cost financially. No longer are insurance companies willing to go along with the obstetrical scam.

Home birth is simultaneously being investigated by insurance companies and it is proving to be safer than and not as costly as hospital deliveries. Insurance companies are impressed by the bottom line of home birth. It is safe, less expensive than hospital birth and appropriate for all healthy women regardless of income. It would be absurd for insurance companies not to want a home birth system in America.

Another reason for hope in a safer birthing system lies in the American families themselves. They are seeing the obstetrical system for what it is and are looking for alternatives. Couples are choosing home birth in greater numbers each year. It is not the low or poverty level income families who are choosing home birth today. Home birth families are well educated, often having technical or scientific backgrounds. They have researched the alternatives and find the scientific birth system to be the safest and healthiest way for them to begin their families. They have stood up to the obstetrical system one family at a time and said, "You are not operating in our best interest. We cannot endanger our lives in your care."

These reasons for hope of a new birthing system encourage me each day. For America is the greatest country in the world. Our strength lies in our ability as a group to admit our mistakes and to change our ways accordingly. We are at a point where even the obstetricians know in their hearts that their system is wrong. The insurance companies know that the system has failed. And our American families are no longer willing to entrust obstetricians with the care of mothers and babies. Fewer and fewer people believe in the present system. So it is simply a matter of time till home birth is reinstated as the most prevalent birthing choice in America. Home birth will return America to its place at the top of the list of industrialized nations where birth is a safe and healthy experience.

To Expectant Families

Football coaches have said of football, and I often say of hospital birth, "We have gotten away from the basics." All the technological advances used today both in professional football and in hospital deliveries are not central to success. For example the Super Bowl is a much more sophisticated game today than ever before. Such advances as radio communication from coach to players during the game, clothing and equipment to increase tremendously the impact a player can endure, and computers and video equipment used to plan strategies for future games are all technological adjuncts. But these adjuncts cannot win a football game if the players are not skilled at blocking and tackling. These basic skills must be strong in order for them to succeed.

Similarly the basics of birth, resulting in a healthy mother and infant, must be in place ahead of all technological adjuncts. The basics: a belief in nature and the body's ability to give birth, support of family and friends for the laboring mother, trust in the medical team, familiar surroundings and comforts of home — these do more to insure healthy delivery than any technological adjuncts ever could. In fact, if the basics are not in place, the use of technological adjuncts send laboring women into a downward spiral leading to cesarean deliveries, birth accidents and the poor bonding of mothers and babies.

For any expectant family, if these basics are not part of a chosen doctor's beliefs about a proper birthing atmosphere then another doctor must be found before birth takes place. It is too late when the expectant mother is in labor to begin questioning the doctor's decisions regarding her case. It is too late for the family to try to intervene in the hospital's birthing system. At this point it is impossible for any new family not to be caught up in the downward spiral of technological interventions, for hospital obstetrics is a complex and deliberately confusing system.

Section One: Homefirst Health Services

To Mothers

It is no longer well known that women are able to give birth. The American obstetrical system has most of us believing that women cannot give birth without obstetricians. They have told the public for too many years that women must be in the obstetricians' sterile locations, with their equipment, and within their time frames in order to give birth. They tell us that if women do not follow their rules then, "something will go wrong."

In reality, they have been guaranteeing that "something would go wrong" for far too many new families. Virtually every woman questioned about her hospital delivery will express disappointment either in her body's inability to give birth, in the lack of skill and compassion of the obstetrical team, or in the baby's inability to nurse in the first days after birth. These disappointments have been accepted by our whole society as simply "the way things are".

But this is so far from the truth!

Women can give birth. They can enjoy giving birth in their own homes. They can give birth without drugs, episiotomies, forceps or C-section surgeries. They can have safe and healthy birth experiences. They can successfully breast-feed their babies. They can give birth vaginally even if they have had cesarean section deliveries in the past.

Home birth empowers women. They can be confident that their bodies will be able to give birth at home. Unlike their disappointed hospital counterparts, home birth mothers will tell you that it was the greatest experience of their lives.

Home Birth Now!

I am pleased to say that the home birth system is in place now in the Chicago area, for healthy women of all economic means to have their babies at home.

My staff and I are pleased to have been a part of so many joyful birthday celebrations over the years. Our home birth families have added to the richness of our lives by sharing with us the beginnings of so many new lives and wonderful new families. We have been privileged to assist at the birth of each and every child we have helped to deliver.

I wish for my readers the courage to defy the present system. I wish you one of life's greatest joys and most incredible miracles — a home birth!

Section Two

Home Birth
Stories

Home Birth Interviews

7

> *Great spirits*
> *have always encountered*
> *violent opposition*
> *from mediocre minds.*
> *— Albert Einstein*

Kathy and her daughter, Colleen
two generations of home birth in Chicago

Kathy first met Dr. Beatrice Tucker when the
doctor was close to 80 years old. Kathy was
pregnant with her first child and had decided
to make the long trip to Maxwell Street's Chicago
Maternity Center to see Dr. Tucker. "The Center was
delivering mostly young mothers from low income neighborhoods and," as Kathy put it, "hippies with long hair
and sandals."

Kathy: I went out of my way to see Dr. Tucker for a
few reasons. I had been seeing another doctor at first

129

early in the pregnancy. Then one day I sat reading the literature in his office which said, "The doctor will give you the anesthetic he has chosen for your needs when he feels you need it." I thought right then, "This is not for me!"

I had three sisters all of whom had babies before me. Two of them had had c-section deliveries and they were already telling me I'd need a c-section because they had needed c-sections. I felt I wanted something different than this. Doctors and their needles had never been my favorite. It seemed that home birth would give me a minimal contact with doctors and no contact with hospitals, which I also feared.

All the hospital delivery stories I had heard were so negative. The only one with a glowing story of birth was my sister's friend. She had wonderful stories of the Chicago Maternity Center. I knew this was for me and I switched over at about 6 months pregnant. The first time I went I remember being put off by the long trip and the location on Maxwell Street. But I felt very good about Dr. Beatrice Tucker.

She was a very serious but likable doctor. I didn't know what an outstanding doctor she was until years later when I read about her in the Chicago Tribune. Dr. Tucker was the first woman obstetrician with a track record for safe delivery of babies. I'm so glad I knew her before she retired from the Chicago Maternity Center.

At the time her style was very different from Dr. Eisenstein's style. Dr. Tucker wanted the home births to be as much like the hospital setting as possible. Two nurses came to my house wearing masks. We all had to

130

wear caps covering our hair. The kitchen had to be covered by plastic sheeting and newspapers. The instruments were sterilized on the stove. I was free to walk around, eat, and do whatever I felt like doing but when the time came to push I has to get up on the kitchen table. They considered the bed to be too soft a place to deliver. She had my husband support me from behind for the delivery.

She made me feel that there was nothing to worry about. I felt confident and had lots of faith in her. As soon as Colleen was born she was put in my arms and we were given some quiet time to get nursing established. Dr. Tucker got me up right away after that. I walked up the stairs to my bedroom shortly after the birth. Follow up visits were made by the Chicago Visiting Nurse Association the next day and the day after that to make sure everything was going all right for both mother and baby.

My husband was very supportive of our home birth plan but everyone else thought I was crazy. At the time insurance wouldn't touch home birth. But at the Chicago Maternity the price of the birth was determined by the zone you lived in. I believe our out of pocket cost was about $100.00.

After Colleen's birth my parents were converted to the idea and were supportive of my other three births. Doctor Tucker announced her retirement during my second pregnancy, but she helped me get established with Dr. Eisenstein, who delivered my next three babies at our home.

It was when I got with Dr. Eisenstein's practice that

I became aware of La Leche League. He really talked up
the benefits of being in the League. With Colleen I had
no support for nursing, but was able to do it successfully. The only problem I had was the flack I took from
from people who told me the baby was too thin. They
would ask me why she was sucking on her hands, surely this meant she was hungry! Even though I had the
doctor's word that she was fine, everyone worried me
about the nursing. So I only nursed her three months.
But later, with Dr. Eisenstein's practice I was very supported and nursed my last two children for four and
four and a half years, respectively.

Colleen (Kathy's daughter), and her husband, Steve

Colleen: Growing up I knew my little sisters had
slept in my parent's bed and that they had been born at
home and nursed for long times, but as a teen this was
nothing you ran around telling people. I saw my sister
being born in 1976 and another sister being born in
1981. I remember Dr. Eisenstein being at the house all
day with the last birth.

The best way to describe my impressions of home
birth as a child was to contrast it with the TV versions
of birth where women were screaming and frightened.
My mom just seemed to manage it. I remember no big
agony and then suddenly there was a baby! I wish I
could have said to people then, "It's not like on TV!"

It wasn't until I was in college and studying about
how to raise children that the facts seemed to speak for
themselves. I felt my mother had been on the right

track. When I first met my husband I remember telling him that I'd have to have my children at home some day. We knew from the first week we met that we wanted to get married and have a family. He seemed fine with the home birth idea.

We did marry and wanted to have a family. It was toward the end of my first pregnancy that we took a birthing class at the local hospital. My husband was in law school and we didn't have the time to get up to Dr. Eisenstein's office for Homefirst's own childbirth class. I remember the instructor from the hospital asking the class, "Who will breast feed?" Hands would go up and she'd respond, "That's noble of you but it doesn't always work." Then she'd ask, "Who wants a natural delivery." To those with hands raised she'd say, "That's noble of you but it is not a failure if you need drugs."

I discovered through this class that, to the hospital staff, natural birth these days really means vaginal birth — with drugs, epidurals, episiotomies, forceps. Our instructor went so far as to say, "There are fifteen couples here. Four of you will have a c-section birth." Next time we have a baby I'd like to go back there just to add a few comments of my own about home birth and nursing.

The hospital plan for a nursing mother sounded like a nightmare. If a baby was born in the night the mother would not see the infant until morning. There were no "rooming in" arrangements for babies. The instructor explained that it was all right to wait until morning to see the baby because the nursery would give them sugar water to make sure they were able to suck. She said it didn't matter that you wouldn't try nursing till morning because the baby would only be getting colostrum for the first few days any way — only colostrum. I couldn't believe it!

They certainly weren't using scientific information in this class or the assistance of La Leche League on matters of nursing. Their advice was so harmful to new mothers!

When Dr. Eisenstein spoke at our last La Leche League Convention I remember him giving a one sentence lecture on the topic of "How to educate your physician on the benefits of breast-feeding." His one sentence was, "No, it can't be done." It certainly felt that was the case in our childbirth class. New mothers have to depend on other nursing mothers in the League for information and support.

If I had had to go to the hospital there would have been a problem as things worked out with my labor. My water bag broke before labor. Homefirst sent me to their Rolling Meadows office for an ultrasound to see if there was still enough amniotic fluid and to check for infection. Everything was fine and I was sent home to wait for labor to start. It was almost 24 hours later that I began to labor.

It was actually quick for a first birth. I had six hours of intense labor. Luckily, it was the opposite of the movie births for me. I was pretty quiet when things got intense and then I felt like pushing. I remember the nurses saying, "The baby will be here before the doctor." And she was right. Emily was born and then the Homefirst doctor rang our doorbell. It was a great, easy first birth.

Right away Emily was put on my chest and we tried nursing. If I would have been in the hospital I know I wouldn't have gotten the instant support I received from the home birth nurses. They were right there with a suggestion to help me get her started nursing properly.

I felt so empowered at home. We got the plan we wanted for our family, not some hospital's outdated plan.

Kathy (Colleen's mother)

Kathy: What I liked about home birth was that you could do whatever you felt like doing — stand up, lie down, take a shower. With one child I felt like delivering on my hands and knees. With Dr. Eisenstein that was all right — whatever felt right at the time.

Home birth seemed so right. Now even more so since I am a volunteer for St. Francis Hospice. Being born at home and dying at home with the people present who love you is the only thing that makes sense. There is no good reason to separate people from their families for birth and death. Those who work with the dying are sometimes called "Midwives to the soul." If you look at it that way, birth and death are so connected.

Steve (Colleen's husband)

Steve: I was nervous, not that we were having a home birth, but that we were having a child. I remember spending a lot of time in the night looking out the window waiting for help to arrive. But now I could deliver the next one if the doctor doesn't get here on time. I know what to expect. Next time we will have more people around for help and more support. The first time we wanted to do it alone. Now that we have had that experience, we know that we want more people around us to share the next event.

Kathy (Colleen's mother)

Kathy: I don't remember which doctor said it, either Dr. Ratner or Dr. Mendelsohn, "If you baby a baby when it's a baby then you don't have to baby the baby for the rest of its life." That always stuck with me and it was certainly true of my children. I bonded with them so strongly when they were little that it worked for me.

I am now a psychologist for the public school system. In my job I do special education evaluations. I'd never say anything, but when I take the health histories of children who started antibiotics at age three months, I often think to myself, "If this child had been breast-fed there wouldn't be a need for antibiotics with all these recurring ear infections."

It seems to get worse every year, the numbers of children with health problems. But I try to remember that I see only those children who need serious help. Sometimes I need to be cheered up after a rough day. Then I come over and visit my granddaughter, Emily."

Jean, a Home Birth Doctor, Has a Home Birth

Dr. Jean was part of the staff of Homefirst Family Health Services, delivering babies at home from 1986 to 1995. A professional position took her husband, Paul, to Pennsylvania in the fall of 1995 and Jean joined him in their new life in Pottstown, Pennsylvania.

Dr. Eisenstein felt that an interview with Dr. Jean would provide very inspirational reading, not only because she was such a beloved member of the Homefirst staff.

These were her comments on Homefirst, Dr. Eisenstein and her recent home delivery.

Jean: Meeting Mayer Eisenstein was a transforming experience for me. I knew I had met a kindred spirit when, after a two hour phone conversation, he hired me on the spot, over the phone. I wasn't sure I had had enough experience delivering babies "on the labor line" during my training at Cook County Hospital. I had probably delivered 30 babies and told Mayer of my uncertainty about not having enough experience to do home births. He responded, "We'll train you!"

I followed Mayer around on his busy schedule that first week and met the other people on the staff. But when I actually went to one of the home births, it was so awesome I was convinced, on the spot, that this was the way to have a baby.

"The labor line" at Cook County had been my only other experience delivering babies and it had been nothing like this home birth! I don't know how many nightmares I had about that labor line! We had to catch the babies before they fell into buckets positioned under each of the "break away" delivery tables, bossed around the whole while by these autocratic obstetrical nurses who would yell at us and make us feel as small as worms. We had to deliver the babies in the "usual" way — episiotomy first, then catch those slick newborns before they fell on the floor or in the buckets. The babies were then whisked away by the nurses while we sewed up the new mothers. It was a nightmare! I can't tell you how many times I dreamed that I missed and the babies were on the floor!

I knew the "labor line" was an extreme way to have a baby. However, I also knew a couple on my volleyball team that summer at Cook County who had delivered their own child at home. Their son was born severely brain damaged and at age six, while strapped into a stroller, would watch us play volleyball. Each of these birthing styles looked like nightmare alternatives. I didn't know there was another way besides these two extremes until I met Mayer.

Some years later, even the birth of my first child, Kate, had been an awful hospital delivery. I had an induced labor, they broke my water bag in the hospital and I had a huge episiotomy. This was not a birthing experience I wanted to repeat.

It was still years later when Kate was enrolled at the Chicago Waldorf School that I happened to notice, in the school's fund raising auction listings, that a home birth with Dr. Eisenstein was one of the items to bid on. This was the most radical thing I had seen! I knew I had to learn more about this. Eventually, it was my accountant, a parent herself having had several home births, who introduced me to Mayer.

I'll never forget that first phone conversation with Mayer. We talked for hours about the politics of practicing medicine. I had always had radical leanings but had no context to put my feelings into practice. Mayer was the first doctor to agree with me that it was a good idea that I had decided not to complete my residency at County due to the negative impact this type of training has on new doctors. Mayer had these same feelings, that the socialization process in that second year is so harmful. No one at a teaching hospital wants to teach you anything if you are interested in family practice. The "first class" students have specialties such as surgery and every one wants to help them out. Those in family practice are made to feel the lowest on the totem pole, and they are treated as orphans in the residency program. I had opted instead to spend one year as an attending at County and then I apprenticed with a family practitioner in Waukegan.

So here was Mayer on the phone, a kindred spirit with a few years more experience under his belt, validating my own thoughts and giving me permission to do and say all the things I had wanted to do and say for years!

I learned a wealth of things from Mayer, from our fellow doctors, and from our patients. It was such a pleasure to practice medicine with a doctor who, like myself, was radicalized about medicine and on such a different path than the one taken by those who had gone all the way through the system before seeing the harm of it. Mayer showed us all such respect. The doctors in his practice shared input about patients. We consulted with each other all the time and Mayer, too, would ask us for advice. This is just not done in other practices.

Perhaps the most important thing I learned from Mayer and his staff was the significance of breastfeeding. Homefirst empowers women not only to deliver their babies naturally but to successfully nurse their infants. This is such an important aspect of health and bonding not stressed in other practices.

A Move to Pennsylvania

It was very sad to leave Homefirst when my husband Paul was hired for a job in Pennsylvania. I had come to love my job and my patients. But Paul had been so unhappy at his Chicago position that I felt it was time for him to try something else. We were a team and his happiness mattered too.

I was recently reminded by a friend that at my going away party in Chicago, I said that I'd probably have to go all the way to Pennsylvania in order to relax from the hectic pace of the home birth practice. I predicted that I'd relax and find myself pregnant. We had wanted a child for years and it did seem feasible that I was carrying around so much concern for my patients that I was unable to conceive my own baby.

We moved to a home in a beautiful region of Pennsylvania. The seasonal changes were fabulous out in the country and my husband loved the gardening possibilities. After a year or so there I had gotten involved in another type of alternative medical practice which I was enjoying very much. However, I was beginning to wake up at 3 a.m. with hot flashes and sweats and the feeling that I must be going through a premature menopause.

On one of our visits to our former neighborhood in Evanston, Illinois, I told Paul that I wanted to stop at Osco to get a pregnancy test. We were staying with friends on our old block of Cleveland Street. We went back to their house and took the test. It was positive!

A Great Pregnancy

When we got back to Pennsylvania I had an ultrasound done. Everything was fine and there on the screen was a ten week old fetus that looked like a gummy bear! I was already through most of the first trimester, didn't even know I was pregnant and was feeling great. It was a great pregnancy, I ate well and exercised and was in good shape to deliver. I was anxious, of course, due to my age. Since I see so many children with handicaps in my Pennsylvania practice, I had a fear of having an abnormal child. I didn't know if I could handle a severe handicap. At the same time I didn't want to have an amniocentesis test done. That particular test can sometimes cause the baby to miscarry and at best it doesn't tell the parents all the possible problems the child might have. My husband, Paul was great through my fearful times. He would respond to my "what ifs" with, "Jean, it's still our baby."

I had a very easy pregnancy, but I did go overdue with this baby. Towards the end of the pregnancy I went to the hospital for a non-stress test. I was armed with the candy bars I had recommended for so many of my patients. Sometimes the consumption of sugar and chocolate will wake up the baby for this test and the mother will spend less time being monitored. They hooked me up to the monitors but my baby slept right through the test. Eventually they gave my belly a "cattle prod" sort of shock which made the baby wiggle around and the test results were fine. They also wanted to schedule another ultrasound to check the amount of amniotic fluid and a stress test in the hospital using an intravenous pitocin drip. The tests were scheduled for Friday and I feared having to go for these particular tests.

Labor

Paul and I discussed the option of trying to get labor to start with the aid of castor oil and some herbs. If it worked we could have the baby before the tests on Friday. After all, Thursday was to be a major astrological event, a lunar eclipse. We had chosen to be married at sunrise on the summer solstice some years back so this seemed a most appropriate beginning for our baby.

The feeling about home birth in Pennsylvania is one of such acceptance due to the large number of Amish living there. The state is much more relaxed and supportive about this choice made by so many Amish over the years. Having mid-wives present at a home birth is widely accepted and even insurance companies support this decision. The attitude is very different from what I had experienced in Illinois.

So, on this beautiful September day, I took the herbs and castor oil suggested by our mid-wives and hoped it would bring about labor.

My friend Christina came over and we did some "soul work" to help me get over the fears I had from my first delivery fourteen years earlier. Another friend, Barbara, who does rhythmical massage therapy, stopped at the house and stayed for dinner. We sat outside and grilled a lovely meal. Barbara had been at many home births and had had some of her own. By this time the castor oil had worked so well that I felt like I was stricken with cholera and labor did start. As I got up from the dinner table my water bag broke. It was 8 p.m. and the lunar eclipse had just started!

Contractions were every two or three minutes. I got into the bath tub and we called the midwives. My friends came over. Christina did some acupuncture on me. Jeanie was at my side the whole time. Jeanie's daughter, nine year old Emily, stood in for my own daughter who was away at school. A certified nurse mid-wife and a registered nurse came from the Reading's Birth and Womens' Center and, of course, Paul was there.

I went to completely dilated very quickly but the hard part was that I pushed for three hours. I was in labor through the whole eclipse. It would have looked pretty funny to an outsider, me walking all through my house stark naked, trying various location and positions for pushing with all these people following behind me. Everybody helped so much. I had wonderful music playing, songs about birth sung by midwives of Sonoma, California and Boulder, Colorado. I was singing along. We played instruments. I was able to get so relaxed between contractions that I could actually fall asleep for a minute in between. It was great!

Michaela is Born!

Our daughter, Michaela Helene, was born at 1:12 a.m. on September 27, 1997 and the eclipse ended at 1:20 a.m. She was so clean and perfect. I had no tearing and hardly any bleeding. She weighed 8 pounds and 12 ounces and was 23 1/2 inches long. We were so thrilled and I was so relieved. It had been exhausting to push for so long!

We did have one innovative procedure performed after her birth. A cord blood specimen was drawn for cryogenic preservation at the Cord Blood Registry (1-888-267-3256.) This is a national organization which preserves cord blood of newborns should the baby or a sibling need these preserved stem cells at a later date in lieu of a bone marrow transplant. There is a sizable fee for the storing of this blood at the registry for your own future use. However, this quick and painless procedure can be done for free at the time of a birth should the parents choose to donate the cord blood for someone else's use. In the case of a family member with an auto-immune disease, such as certain cancers, the blood will be drawn and designated for that family recipient at no charge. I feel it is a tragedy to let this tremendous resource go untapped and hope that more people begin to ask for the harvesting of these healing cells.

After the cord blood draw and knowing that all was well, our friends left pretty quickly so that we could rest. There we were — all in the same bed at home. We tried to sleep but we were pretty excited. Paul got up very early that morning and started making phone calls to family and friends. I can't imagine having a baby any other way!

It is really a wonderful memory.

The Importance of Breastfeeding

As I said before, one of the most important aspects of working with Homefirst was that I learned so much about the importance of breastfeeding. As things developed with my own baby in the first few weeks I needed the help of a lactation consultant to successfully nurse. Since I had had a breast reduction surgery performed at the age of 20, long before I anticipated nursing a baby, I wondered how this would affect breast-feeding. I had not successfully nursed my first baby but I had hopes that the second time around would be better. I did go to a La Leche League meeting before my birth as I always tell patients to do. At the meeting I got some names of people to talk with should I need to consult with them after the delivery.

After the baby was born we were afraid we had "a real pistol" on our hands. If she was awake she was unhappy and always fussing. We were constantly rocking and holding her. I went in for a first check up and she had not lost much weight but by the second check up she had lost about a pound and a half. My concern was that she had wet diapers but no bowel movements for two days. This can be a sign that the baby is not getting enough fat in the diet. For some reason I was able to provide proteins but not enough fat in the hind milk. It is the protein part of the milk that provides the beneficial antibodies to the baby so, I was glad she was getting this part. We don't know why the fats weren't being delivered in the milk, maybe the ducts were plugged from the surgery I had years ago.

At two weeks after the birth I went to see a lactation consultant. I didn't tell her I was a doctor. I didn't want her to leave anything out, assuming I already knew the information because I was a doctor. She got me on the supplemental nursing system (sns) so that the baby could get enough fat in her diet from the formula; yet, still be a nursing baby for the other benefits that I was able to provide. It really worked very well. She turned into a calm baby instantly as a result.

Michaela simultaneously nurses from the breast and from a bottle of formula I wear around my neck with a fine tubing leading from the bottle into her mouth as she nurses. You can even get various sizes of tubing and you can control the flow. It comes out slowly so that, as with nursing, she has to work hard to get the milk out. This system works very well for us.

I'd Do it All Again

I now believe it would be worth nursing this way even if nothing were coming out from the breast because the relationship between the mother and baby is so different from that of a bottle-fed baby and mother. The snuggly, face to face type of feeding is so important. I feel like nursing this baby has been one of the major accomplishments of my life. Really! I had to do so much to get to the point of successful nursing. She is now over twenty pounds at seven months and has been very healthy and calm.

People at airports and in restaurants always want to know what it is I am doing with this bottle around my neck. I explain it to them and so many women say they wish they had known about this when they were nursing. I don't mind explaining because I might be informing someone who could really benefit from this nursing option. Even if they don't need the sns, some women who aren't sure that they can nurse a baby might hear my story and be led to a lactation consultant who could help them to breast feed when they thought it was not possible.

I'd do it all again. It has been very beneficial to both of us!

Sue

Sue has been affiliated with Homefirst for many years, as a patient , office worker and later as a birth nurse and birth teacher.

Section Two: Home Birth Stories

Sue: I was pregnant for the first time when I was twenty years old. I was single and I really wanted the baby. For a twenty year old, I have to say, I did my homework. I determined that my needs were simple, I wanted two things in this birth experience: no drugs unless I was fully informed as to why I needed them (I didn't expect to need any) and I didn't want the baby taken away from me to a nursery. Back then in the hospitals it was routine for the babies to be taken away from the mothers for the first 12 to 24 hours for observation.

Shopping for a Doctor

I spent the first five months of my pregnancy going from doctor to doctor. I'd say to them, "I'd like to do this naturally." And they would say, "You can try it naturally as long as you can handle it." I'd then ask who would decide if I was handling it or not. They would say, "Of course, we know about birth and we will determine if you are handling it without drugs." I'd then leave the office and never go back. I was starting to think there wouldn't be any place for me to have this baby.

A friend of mine had a home birth around this time. At first I thought this was odd but then I realized she did have both of my criteria — she had no drugs for the birth and the baby was not taken away from her. So I went to the Chicago Maternity Center to check out this option. It was a clinic that had been in existence for about a hundred years. It was the typical clinic. A hun-

148

dred people would also be waiting there, all with eight o'clock appointments. But they were the home birth experts and were very supportive of the things I wanted.

Dr. Tucker and the Chicago Maternity Center

It was a hassle to go to Maxwell Street but I was feeling very comfortable with this idea. Just about every medical student in Chicago did a rotation through the Chicago Maternity Center. It was used as a teaching center and new doctors went there to learn how to deliver babies. I remember when I first told my mother that I had decided on a home birth. She started to cry and took out her check book. She thought the only reason I'd do a home birth must be financial.

At about six months along they discovered that my baby was in a breech position so I became a" teaching tool" at the clinic. They had me coming every week so that every medical student going through their rotation could see me. I didn't have ultrasound at that time but I had "x-ray pelvimitry", a series of x-rays sizing my pelvis a few weeks before my due date. That would never be allowed now. Due to the breech position of my baby, I sometimes saw Dr. Tucker herself at the appointments instead of just the interns and residents.

I remember her saying to me, "Honey, breech is just a slight variation of normal." She didn't think it was a big deal and that transferred to me. Friends would comment that they had heard breech birth was a more painful delivery and I'd reassure them that it was just "a slight variation of normal."

149

On one of my last visits to the clinic, before my due date, a medical student, David A., asked if he could come to my birth because he had never seen a breech delivery. He told me to ask for him when the time came. For some reason I have never forgotten his name. Everyone at the Center, including this medical student, expected a long, slow labor since I did not have a head pressing on my cervix.

I Was in Labor

I was living in a sort of commune situation at the time with a lot of other women. One of them had had a baby already. Every day we were ready for my baby to be born. Finally thirteen days after my due date, as one of the other women was sitting in the kitchen I kept getting up to go past her to the bathroom. I didn't think this could be labor starting. I just thought I was having diarrhea. The third or forth time I walked past her she suggested we time these trips to the bathroom. Sure enough, the trips were five minutes apart.

I was so excited about being in labor! But thinking this would be a very long breech labor, I decided to go to the grocery store. Everyone had been joking that this would be such a party when they came to deliver this baby that I had better have some good food in the house. I did fine on the walk to the store but on the way back I was having to stop and sit on people's porches during contractions.

When I got home I decided to call the doctors. They came over and I was already at 5 cm. I was very pleased because this was getting pretty uncomfortable. Then they did what was standard practice in 1972. I was shaved and was given an enema just as if I were in the hospital. Dr. Tucker believed in bringing the hospital atmosphere to the home. They covered my bed in newspaper but I was instructed that I would deliver on the kitchen table when the time actually came.

The next time they checked me they said I could already push. I couldn't believe it was already happening because I expected such a long labor. I pushed for an hour and a half. As I pushed a nurse did something I had never seen before or since. She held the baby's arms down by pushing on the outside of my belly so that the baby wouldn't put her arms up and get her head entrapped. I remember that part didn't feel too good. As she delivered feet first, her head was still in my pelvis and we could already hear her crying. She was fully out a few seconds later — a healthy girl, 6 lb. 5 oz. — and I got to hold her right away.

I felt so good that I had gotten what I wanted. No one offered me drugs throughout my delivery. They did, however, in trying to bring the hospital to my home, hang an iv drip from a nail on the kitchen wall to administer demerol. I had had this natural delivery and then they gave me drugs in order to manually remove the placenta which I retained after the birth. That part was very much like a hospital procedure.

I didn't realize until three years later, when I had my son, that this hadn't really been a "home" birth. But it was as close to one as I could have had in 1972. By 1973 Dr. Tucker had retired and another director was in

charge of the Chicago Maternity Center. There were
fewer and fewer medical students being trained there
due to an emphasis on hospital birth. It became quite a
political issue. Despite a full patient load at the Center it
was determined by the hospital powers-that-be that no
one wanted home birth any more. I remember going to
meetings in protest of the closing. But all the picketing
and petition signing did nothing because Chicago
Maternity Center stopped delivering babies at home.
They had lost their battle to stay open due to the coming
of the Prentice Womens Hospital and a new focus on
hospital delivery for everyone.

Shopping for a New Doctor

By the time I was pregnant with my second child, I
didn't know what I'd do. Dr. Tucker was retired and,
much as before, I went from doctor to doctor and could-
n't get past the interview where I'd tell them I had had a
home birth and would like to have another. No doctor
would give me the support I wanted. I remember touring
the "innovative" maternity floor of Illinois Masonic
Hospital but when I saw the leather straps in the delivery rooms for womens legs and arms I nearly passed
out. My husband was embarrassed but I knew I couldn't
do a hospital delivery with this medieval equipment
around me.

Finally the universe was in harmony one week,
when I was six months pregnant. Two people gave me
Dr. Eisenstein's card that same week. As soon as I went
to see him I knew I had come home. I was comfortable

152

again! I could do this! They were willing to take me even though I was so far along in the pregnancy.

This time my due date was July 27th. I expected to be overdue again. But on July 23 after a full day of working, having a little friend over for my daughter to play with, carrying lots of groceries up to the third floor, and making dinner, I began to have contractions which I assumed were just Brackston-Hicks. It was only after getting into the bath tub that I realized this was really regular labor and this baby wouldn't be overdue like the last. By midnight I told my husband this was it and we called the doctor and all the people we wanted to have at the birth. Mayer was delivering another baby at the hospital that particular night. When we spoke on the phone I could hear encouragement in the background for some pregnant woman ready to push.

Dr Eisenstein Comes to Our House

At the time Dr. Elvove was doing a rotation with Dr. Eisenstein so they both came out to the house. It was about 100 degrees that night. Everyone was dripping sweat but I didn't notice since I was occupied with labor. At one point the doctors were on our back porch, eating stuffed pepper leftovers. I came out from the bedroom and said, "I think maybe you need to check me." He said "Really?!" And I said, "Really!!"

That was at 2 o'clock in the morning. He checked and I was complete. I pushed and Chris was born by 2:21 a.m., weighing in at 9 pounds and 8 ounces. I had no tears, no stitches, no episiotomy. It was amazing.

Section Two: Home Birth Stories

This was a real home birth.

I kept expecting Dr. Eisenstein to "do medical things" to me that night but he never did. I learned that at home the mother needs good medical support but none of the usual hospital procedures such as the shaving and the enema and the IV's. I was convinced that this was the right way to have a baby. So convinced that Home First was called to our next two home births also.

Home Birth is Just So Right

As I was raising my young family I became an exercise teacher for pregnant women, a child birth instructor for Homefirst, the mother of four children and eventually a nurse. Now I assist at births in a hospital setting as a nurse. These are my patients now and it is this job that pays the bills. But it is still the home birth classes and home deliveries that spiritually make me feel so good. Home birth is just so right.

Upstairs, Downstairs

The story of two friends, Therese and Anne and their home births

Anne: Therese and I met at St. Ignatius High School in Chicago. We got to know each other at the new teacher orientation that year and became work friends. I was the school librarian and Therese was in the religion department. We lived in close proximity in Rogers Park and would drive to St. Ignatius together. During that first year Therese's apartment was burglarized twice. She had shared her fears with me on our drives back and forth from school. I knew she was looking for a safer place to live and as it happened the family living upstairs of us in our two flat moved out. So by February she had moved in to our building and by June of 1987 Therese married Tom.

Opposite Experiences

Therese: "Anne had just miscarried. Now that we were living in the same building we were in the habit of taking long walks together. We would talk about work and about our lives on these walks. We had discussed Anne's feelings about the miscarriages she had been through and many other things. By September on one of our walks I told Anne that we were pregnant and I didn't know how it had happened."

Anne: "I think I called her on that point!"

Therese: "Tom and I, by now, had no jobs and no money and just weren't prepared for our own news. Anne and I talked about how we were put into this child thing together, either having a child or losing a child around the same time. There was a real graciousness between us about the whole thing. Anne had experienced a loss and I was sensitive to her loss. At the same time Anne was very sensitive to how we were pregnant and going through the surprise, fears, and changes that an unexpected pregnancy brings. The two of us were living through opposite experiences on those walks. But there really wasn't a feeling of jealousy between us just a real gracious caring. Years later, the tables were turned and I was to miscarry while Anne was pregnant.

At the time I remember real disappointment and concern on Anne's part that maybe they wouldn't be able to have a child. But Anne was very level about it. She taught me through her acceptance of the situation and through her hopeful persistence that they would have a baby some day. Later Anne was so empathetic when I miscarried a baby between my two children's births. We sat on the floor and cried together. I was so grateful that even the miscarriage happened at home. I learned about the womb being a home for life and sometimes for death. Anne was very helpful in my letting go of that baby. Her own level attitude helped me so much.

Andrew's birth

Therese: But back to the story of my first pregnancy. Tom and I began looking into a home birth with Homefirst. We went for a consultation with Dr. Eisenstein about a home delivery and of course, I talked about it with Anne on our walks. We talked about how everyone was thinking we were insane to do something like home birth. Tom and I felt good about the idea, so good that we didn't explore anything else and proceeded to take the birthing course at the Homefirst office.

One Sunday morning in June my water bag broke at about 6 a.m. I didn't know if that was good or bad so we called Homefirst. They said to start walking around. It was Father's Day so we walked as far as church and decided to go in. I was thinking it would be great to have a baby on Father's Day. In our excitement we started to call people when we got home to tell them this was the day. My mother was in the middle of having a party for 25 people at her home in Delaware. She left her own party immediately to fly to Chicago for the birth of her grandchild. My sister also flew in. We thought the baby would surely be here by lunch time.

However, there was slow progress until 4 p.m. We made a birthday cake for the baby. Kay, a physician's assistant from Homefirst came to check on us. Little did we know she would be with us for 33 hours! But Kay knew this would take a long time. Labor was strong and progress slow. Several doctors conferenced by phone about our case and at 11 p.m. I went to sleep. It was then that labor started intensely and Anne was invited to come upstairs with us. I don't remember much about the next day except that it was 106 degrees outside. Anne and Tom didn't leave my side all day. They iced me down all day and night. I never felt the heat! I could just cry every time I think about how faithful they were. I'll never forget that.

By now the feelings were so deep that around 8:30 at night I said, 'I can't do this! Give me heroin, anything!' I could hardly speak. By 9 p.m. I felt the baby's head come out and I rallied. It was great. Anne was holding up one of my legs and another friend, Michelle, had the other one. With Tom supporting me from behind I felt so secure. After about two pushes Andrew was here!

Ann: When I look back on it everything was fine. I do have the memory of being scared, but I had never been at a birth. This was just the way things proceed sometimes at births. And Therese was really fine all along. She expected no trouble and had no fears. She did it without medication.

Therese: There are six children in my family. I remember that those not present with us were involved from a distance calling in on the phone. My mother was so excited that around the time of the birth she stretched the 20 foot phone cord into the hall outside my room. My brother, Kevin was able to hear the baby being born all the way in Delaware. He then relayed the excitement to the rest of the family via his own car phone. He was yelling the news to his girlfriend in his car and she was passing the details on to the rest of the brothers on the other end of her phone call. Even his neighbors were getting the details as he yelled my progress out the window, "She is at 10 centimeters!" and "The baby's head is out!"

Anne: It was absolutely an awesome miracle. And such a relief that all was ok. It was my first home birth to witness. The Homefirst staff was wonderful. This first experience of birth changes you for life. I understood about birth after that. I understood enough so that when I had my children there weren't any surprises about the process.

Christiana's birth

Anne: During my pregnancy with Christiana I felt fine and everything was normal. But towards the end I developed slightly high blood pressure. When I was two

158

weeks overdue I went in for stress and non-stress tests. I was fine and so was the baby but they told me I could go only one more week over my due date without intervention. One week later there were no signs of labor and the baby was still high. I went with Dr. Jean of Homefirst to Weiss Hospital to have labor induced with the help of the drug, pitocin. Even after 11 hours of a pitocin drip there were no cramps and there was no significant labor.

I remember being so disappointed that this wasn't going to work. The doctors at Weiss recommended a c-section. So Christiana was born that night at 10:45 p.m. with no complications or problems. She wasn't a huge baby after being so-called three weeks late. She weighed 7 lbs. 9 oz. And I recovered easily.

Therese: Christiana was a beautiful baby. I remember the disappointment prior to going to Weiss Hospital. Anne was very upset about having to leave home but she was so pleased about the treatment given her at Weiss and so pleased with the baby.

Anne: I had set myself up for only one way of giving birth, at home. But I integrated it all pretty quickly afterwards since the baby was fine.

Annelise's birth

Anne: Eight months later I was pregnant with our second child. That pregnancy went well and now Therese and I were both pregnant and due two months apart. This baby was due April 14, however I expected that she would be a week later. This time I had no blood pressure problem. However, when I was still pregnant into the third week of May (now 6 weeks late in delivering) I had to go back for some tests again, stress and non-stress tests. The results were all fine and I was feeling ok.

Finally, on a Saturday I woke up and told Chris, "It might be today!" I got up and walked around and began having regular labor pains. Therese came downstairs and we walked and talked but didn't call the doctors till around 11 a.m. It was nice. Labor was steady. Because of my history with labor I was mostly concerned that the doctor would come to check my progress and tell me I had no progress. However, he said I was already at 5 cm. I continued to walk and Therese rubbed my back till around 3:30 p.m. By then I felt I could no longer be on my feet.

Therese: She was great. She progressed so calmly.

Anne: My mother took Christiana to her house. Then there were two hours of pushing with lots of slow stretching of the peritoneal area with special oils brought by Dr. Paul of Homefirst. Pushing was slow and incremental but Paul was great with the stretching techniques to avoid tearing. The baby was so large (10 lb. 3 oz.) that it really helped. She was born in our bed with Chris supporting me from behind.

Annelise came out blue and not breathing correctly. The birth had been textbook correct, however, she didn't look good at birth. They rubbed her back and put her on portable oxygen — completely different from Andrew's birth which I had witnessed. Finally the doctor did give her to me to hold. The baby was holding her own but

160

did need to be transferred to the hospital for observation and oxygen. For some reason I remained calm. I knew this was the best place for her to be watched. We had cake for her and soon an ambulance came to take her to Evanston Hospital. I felt she was in good hands.

By morning we went to see her in the intensive care unit for infants. There she was, all 10 lb. 3 oz of her surrounded by truly ill newborns weighing two or three pounds. She was now pink and off oxygen and fine. Dr Paul came to help us get the nursing process started and she was fine after that. I didn't spend any time thinking that her late birthdate had any thing to do with her breathing problems. It was just one of those things that can happen and we were well cared for in the face of it.

Therese: Thank goodness she had been receiving oxygen from her cord all along. Dr. Paul was so great. He made good, quick decisions. We did feel safe with him there. And the story had a great outcome.

Caitlin's birth

Therese: This time labor started in the night. It was intense and very brief. Kay from Homefirst came over about 4 a.m. and did an exam. At about 4:30 I started yelping and by 6 a.m. she was born. She came so fast my friend called her "a shooting star". She was 8 lb. 4 oz.

Anne: She came out like a runaway freight train!

Therese: I remember thinking that this couldn't be happening so fast! It was so different from the days of labor I had with Andrew. I looked fine in the photos afterwards because I hadn't gone through hours of labor this time.

That morning was the only one of Andrew's life when he slept in. He usually woke up at 6 a.m. but on this day he slept till 8 a.m. He came out of his room with his blanket and there was a baby! Right away he handed Caitlin his prized possession, his "baa boo"(blanket). This time Anne wasn't in the photos because she took all of the pictures for us.

Anne: We bought a cake for Caitlin because there wasn't time to make one!

The Final Piece of Growing Up

Anne: Being friends and in the same building for all our births was such a blessing.

Therese: And we didn't know what we were getting into! At first I was just chatting with a work friend about having been robbed and here we are — four babies later!

Anne: We did that final piece of growing up together.

Therese: Even the miscarriages were a part of it all, processing all those feelings on the walks to the park. I look back and see that I was just so scared when I was pregnant the first time. Anne had just had her miscarriages and was still able to help me through being young and unexpectedly pregnant.

It was wonderful to go through pregnancy and birth, nursing and early parenthood with a good friend.

Anne: It was a blessing!

Tom and Chris, the Upstairs Downstairs Fathers, and their perspective

Tom: I felt pretty comfortable with the idea of home birth from the start. Then after listening to Dr. Eisenstein's information session, hearing the conscientiousness with which Homefirst supported the parents and knowing they had a back up system in place — I felt they knew what they were doing.

This was not the case for my in-laws and my parents. They were pretty upset about our choice. Even as Therese was in labor I received a phone call from my brother-in-law in Delaware urging us to go to the hospital and be done with this "non-sense."

Chris: I thought it sounded great to be at home, to never leave your house. That is what has been done for ages and ages. I was very comfortable with the idea when Anne said she'd like to have the baby at home.

Tom: For dads there is such a feeling of excitement about home birth but also a feeling of helplessness. We dads get trained to help the mothers get through some of the pain but it is not easy. It is frustrating at times because you wish you could do more to help. For us we had some of Therese's closest women friends with us, the clan of women, who had been through this before.

That was good and I was glad for it but I felt a bit marginalized by it, also. They had been through this experience and I hadn't. I had a feeling of helplessness along with the excitement. I wasn't worried however, and was in a reasonable comfort zone all along. With Andrew's birth I just wondered when it was going to happen.

I remember falling asleep for about an hour and a half over those two days of labor. I woke up with this feeling of, "Where am I? What is happening?" Then I heard Therese moaning and had the dread feeling, "Oh no, we still have no baby!" That was frustrating.

And the next birth was so different. We expected the 40 hours of labor again. But with our second birth I began to mark the length of time between the contractions. After about twenty minutes I said, "Forget this! These contractions are coming fast and furiously."

Whereas with the first birth I had pages and pages, days of contractions recorded. Their births and the children themselves are so different! I guess that is the way they all are.

Chris: I have to agree with Tom. Dads go to these classes and are informed about what we can do to make the mothers more comfortable but there is a feeling of helplessness. All you can do is encourage the mother to relax, let her rest on you, do back rubs, cold towels on the forehead. But the women have to go through the pain of it.

With Christiana's birth, when we had to transfer to the hospital, I very much felt I had to weigh the pros and cons. I wanted to make the best decision for the child. Do we go home and wait or have the c-section? As the father you don't know if it is safe to wait or if you should listen to the doctors at the hospital. They don't want to play a waiting game with you and you don't want to put your child in danger. It was a difficult decision once we were transferred to a hospital. As a father

164

that helplessness is the hard part.

At least when Annelise was born at home and came out looking the wrong color, we felt we had expert advice this time between Dr. Paul and the nurse from Homefirst. It wasn't that the baby was in grave danger, but Dr. Schauttauer felt she needed observation at the hospital. We felt supported by Homefirst and not so helpless.

I remember too, the feeling with the first baby that I wasn't sure what I would do, how I would react as a father for the first time. I had never been enamored with other people's babies. But with Christiana, as soon as she was born all my feelings changed instantly. I knew as soon as I held her that I'd be capable of loving and nurturing this tiny person. By the time we had Annelise there was no question, being a father was the normal thing to do.

Tom: I'd say that there is less anxiety at home births for the fathers than there is in the hospital. You know your home — it's your home! You don't have to go to an antiseptic and bureaucratic place with a lot of strangers. I know I felt that as a man. And how much more a woman feels it with this sacred event happening.

It was just really all of a flow. You are at home. You work, have dinner, feel contractions, report in. Then the doctor comes. It felt smooth and eliminated anxiety.

When you have a home birth it becomes a reality for you, it feels like the norm. But in talking to friends sometimes you realize this is certainly not the norm for them.

I remember at a party telling a couple that both our

children were born at home. They had several children but never heard of home birth. They felt this was so alien. At the same time I was so surprised to hear that home birth was so unfathomable to them because in our own subculture it was the only way to go. We were really surprising each other.

Chris: It is amazing how the thinking has changed in so short a time, really. It is only in the last hundred years or so that babies have been born in the hospital. The hospital is the unnatural place to have children, not home. I guess some people prefer the quickness of going to the hospital and having interventions in the labor process. Some people we know actually prefer c-sections to labor — it gets the job over and done with. But they don't take into account that when those drugs wear off it hurts and it's hard to move around. I remember it was even hard for Anne to get out of bed for a few days.

Humans are funny that way sometimes. They can take a perfectly natural event and make a big deal about it. That is what intelligence can do for us. I grew up on a farm in Poland. My three brothers and I were all born at home. The midwife came when the contractions were a short time apart. Within an hour or two the baby was born. I think after every one of us my mother was back in the fields the next day. She went back to the chores because she was needed on a small farm. The whole thing was very matter of fact.

When we told them about our idea of having a home birth, my parents were fine with it. It was all they knew!

Tom We are moving soon to an area of Pennsylvania where there are lots of Amish people. There will be no problem having a baby at home there. It is the norm.

Our next baby is due in the fall. We will just have to assume that with our great track record so far we will be able to find similar care in Pennsylvania. It will be without Homefirst and without our friends this next time, and that is a concern. We have been well cared for in Chicago.

Twins at Home!

*An interview with new mother, Kim
She and her husband, Larry, had their twins at
home December 27, 1996.*

They were the 6th set of twins delivered at home by Homefirst in 1996 and the first set of boy/girl twins.

Kim: When I was first pregnant with the twins, of course I didn't know that they were twins. I mentioned in my aerobics class that I'd like to find out about having the birth at home. To my surprise people came out of the woodwork with information for me. Someone gave me Dr. Eisenstein's book to read, *The Home Court Advantage.* I read it in one sitting and loved it. We went to a consultation with Dr. Eisenstein and we were sold. My mother was at first uncertain of this idea but she knew we were serious and had done our research on the topic. She was reassured by all the medical equipment brought to the home by the Homefirst doctors who attend the birth. She wanted to be sure that if something was going wrong the doctors would be prepared.

In my second trimester I was larger than I should have been at that point. An ultrasound was done which showed two babies. There are twins in the family so we were surprised but not surprised and very happy. My pregnancy went without a hitch due to our main focus on calories, nutrition and fluids to support the babies. Friends would tell us that we could count on the babies being early because twins just don't make it to term. My own sister had had twins 6 weeks early delivered by c-section. So we were careful to focus on all the supports we could implement to provide good health for me and the babies.

My due date was December 29 and much to our delight they were born full term on December 27. I was so pleased that I was able to do that for them! We had quite a support team at the house that day. My sister and mother were there, two nurses from Homefirst, Janita and Christie; a friend studying to be a doctor of naprapathy, Dr. Mark and Dr. Eisenstein, a friend assigned to videotape the event and two of our own sons.

Why Didn't We Do This Before?

The first nurse to check my progress said I was at 4 cm. Our friend studying to be a doctor did foot massages for me and I was able to relax in the tub with essential oils. There wasn't really any significant pain and within two hours I was up to 8 cm. When Drs. Mark and Eisenstein came I wondered when things would pick up in intensity. It was 11 p.m. and we were still just visiting with each other. My husband and I went alone into our finished basement to see if labor would pick up in a quiet "regrouping" space. I remember thinking that if this was home birth why hadn't we don't this before! I was at 9 cm by then and doing fine. After a shower by 1 a.m. I went to bed to rest.

In the morning there were still no babies and everyone looked so tired. I thought that I should feed people but my husband said I shouldn't worry about anyone else. I am that type of person, trying to make everyone comfortable in my house. By 9 a.m. Dr. Eisenstein discussed what could be done to move us along in this labor. He decided there were too many people there for me to be concerned about. I was worried that I had kept all these people up for too long. Dr. Eisenstein gave me a packet of carbohydrates used for athletes with a large amount of water.

At this point I knelt on the couch and leaned over the back of it. Dr. Mark asked if I felt that I could push at all. The contractions were getting heavier but I was waiting for that awful back labor I had in the hospital with previous births. I was having no back labor at all this time but it had been a large part of my hospital births. My husband helped me get through a few heavier contractions. Then Dr. Mark checked and there was a head already! With about 8 seconds of pushing our daughter was born. I couldn't believe it! They put her on my chest and she nursed right away. And only 13 minutes later our son shot out so fast it was lucky Janita was there to catch him. My sister was videotaping and later said she felt like throwing down the camera and running over to catch the baby when he flew out so fast.

Easiest Labor

This was my easiest labor. I had no sutures and no episiotomy as I had had with my hospital births. We were so thrilled. Holly weighed 6lb.15 oz. and Timothy weighed 6 lb. 5 oz. Each of them was 19 1/2 inches long and perfectly healthy! I would do it again at home in a minute. It was great! My sister's twins came over and were able to hold our twins. Everything was just perfect.

Being a nurse myself I thought all along it was best to try to have twins at home because I know what happens in the hospital. It wasn't so much that I would have been uncomfortable or frightened there but the intervention would have been awful. With Homefirst I only had 2 ultrasounds and 2 non-stress tests to see how things were progressing. I had so much less intervention this way. Most mothers carrying twins are scheduled for c-sections. It is assumed that things will go wrong so no one has a fair trial in labor to see if they can deliver their own babies.

We felt that Homefirst had the scientific knowledge of what should be done in this situation, supported by research and experience. It was a comfortable and safe way to give birth. We could see that Dr. Eisenstein, himself, was so pleased with our births! As he left our house he remarked about how happy he was at having assisted twins into the world that day.

Peggy, Home Birth After Cesarean

Peggy: Our first child, Patrick, intended to be a home birth with Homefirst but at two weeks late, in a breech position, with no hope of turning from his high up position, a c-section delivery was done. Generally c-sections are not done on Homefirst patients without a trail of labor at home, but Patrick was so stuck it seemed unfair, in Dr. Jean's opinion, to wait for labor knowing the outcome would be a cesarean birth any-way. So Patrick was delivered at Weiss Memorial Hospital by their surgeons with Dr. Jean present and all went well.

I Wasn't the Least Bit Worried

Two years later when I become pregnant with our second child, Maura, no one at Homefirst was the least bit concerned that I had had a previous c-section deliv-ery. All the reasons for Patrick's c-section were non-repeating reasons. I, too, was not the least bit worried. I wasn't even going into the pregnancy dreading labor because I had not been in labor before and didn't know what that feeling would be like. I knew we wouldn't have an automatic second c-section with Homefirst, so I was-n't anticipating that complication again. I was, in a sense, like a first time mom. We were unsure if this labor would progress like a first time labor or a second. This we could deal with.

Actually, when the time came, we did have a rather long first time labor. When we put Patrick to bed around

171

9:30 that evening I didn't know if my cramps were labor or not. When we called Dr. Jean she told us that things were too erratic so far and that we should try to get some sleep. By 6 a.m. labor had become regular but not too intense. We called Homefirst again and by 7:30 a.m. the nurse from Homefirst came to our house. She said things looked good so we decided to get on with our day. We took care of our son, did some jobs around the house and by noon Dr. Jean arrived.

My sister from down the block took little Patrick to play at his cousin's house.

We had completed the Bradley Childbirth refresher course this time. However, with our first child, we had not experienced any of the labor, breathing, or pushing we had learned about. This was really a first time experience and, as it turned out, the Bradley method helped a lot.

My husband, Patrick, the Homefirst staff, and I were able to sit around most of the day telling stories to each other and having a pleasant visit. Every once in a while I'd hold on to the wall until a contraction passed and all was fine. I never felt it was unbearable or frightening or impossible to manage. I felt I could do it this time, remembering from the Bradley class, "Every contraction, one at a time, brings the baby closer to birth." So I really felt the purpose of labor.

That Whole Day Was So Nice

What I was afraid of was that my bed would break with so many people on it at one time. We had decided to hang out in the upstairs bedroom with the staff drifting in and out as needed. That whole day was so nice. We did what we wanted to do. The staff was available, but they sensed when to drift in and out keeping a distance from us sometimes and being at my side when I needed them. I never got to where I felt that I would need medication to control the pain.

Our neighbor, Pam Bradley, had offered their hot tub for my use when they found out we were in labor. The heat in the tub had been dialed up and by about 5:30 p.m. it was ready for use. This was an idea supported by our doctors and nurses who knew there can be great labor relief in water, but by this time I knew I didn't want to leave the upstairs.

I got into the bath tub at home and my husband poured cups of hot water over my belly for relief. This was great until our hot water tank ran out of hot water. As I got out of the tub Dr. Jean told me I could now try pushing. But I never felt like pushing through the whole experience. I expected this great urge to push and that such relief would come from pushing, but that sensation never came. This was puzzling and made it seem like the baby would never come. I pushed for hours — in our bed, standing up, in different rooms.

Maura, 9 lb., 3 oz.!

Finally she was born, with so many people on our bed at once: me, my husband Patrick, Dr. Jean, the two nurses and a visiting doctor from Homefirst. It was not easy. I kept waiting for this great urge to push. I was expecting the baby to push out even if I didn't want to push. This stage was very hard work.

Maura was 9 lb. 3 oz. — a good size for a first vaginal birth. It was great to see her and her birth certainly set me up for an easier subsequent home birth two years later. I needed no episiotomy. Labor had gone well! My husband was comfortable all the time with Maura's birth. He was there to cut her cord and was simply amazed by the whole process. The Homefirst staff had been so helpful by exuding nothing but confidence in my ability the whole time.

After Maura was weighed we had cake and champagne. Soon her brother, Patrick, came home from my sister's house. His eyes were so wide. He was very enamored with this new little person. It had all worked so well.

Are You Sure About This?

My family had been so concerned that once I had a c-section I would need another one. In all the 27 births of my siblings' children the only c-section had been mine. They were so worried that I'd die at home in need of another c-section. My sister who has eight children brought me a wicker bassinet used by all her babies. It was a few days before our due date and she was still saying, "Are you sure about this?" She is a mother who, in labor, calls ahead to the hospital warning them to set up the epidural. She is on the way!

Within a half hour after Maura's birth I called this sister to say, "I'm in my bed with my daughter in my arms and we're all fine!"

When she came to visit us, my sister with eight births of her own noted that she never had such great after-care in the hospital as we got from Homefirst in our own home.

Lots of people thought we were nuts. In fact, we didn't tell many people about our plans, not wanting the extra conflict. We were pleasantly surprised when we told Patrick's parents that Maura had been born at home. They thought it was a fine idea and even knew one of the nurses with Homefirst.

In one sense I was very determined to have a home birth. In my very large family I am one of the youngest. My brothers and sisters often think of me as a kid and themselves as the adults. When they objected to home birth it was like waving a red flag in front of the charging bull. I became even more determined to prove that home — birth works!

Don't Look at Pregnancy as Illness

My youngest sister, who lives down the street from us, was pregnant with her first child when we were expecting little Patrick. My sister was due before me and we were sad to watch every intervention possible happen to her in the hospital and it all happened so routinely. We knew we didn't want this to happen to us too.

In our reading about the Bradley method we learned that you have to chose your own style of delivery before walking in the door if you are going to go to a hospital for labor and delivery. You can't let them set you up first with an IV line, then a hospital gown, then pitocin, then a fetal monitor. When they set you up to be a patient then you are set up to accept more and more layers of intervention. If you allow them to view your condition as a sickness then you need them to "cure" you. But if you don't look at pregnancy as an illness then you don't ever have to go to the hospital to get "cured."

Lifeguards

I remember an analogy Dr. Eisenstein uses to describe home birth. It said that you can certainly swim without a lifeguard present but it is good to have one around should you need a lifeguard. If any couple is going to have a baby they should be able to birth the baby but it is advisable to have someone knowledgeable on hand should a situation arise that requires help.

I really thought about that idea a lot. One hundred years ago there weren't options as there are today for birthing babies. But with all our modern options and equipment, why not choose the healthier, easier, safer, more personal, more dignified way to deliver a baby with less intervention and ultimately less pain.

I remember being curled up in a ball on the table waiting for the specialist to insert a needle in my spine before Patrick's delivery. It was miserable for me at nine months pregnant to hold this position and I wasn't even in labor. I can't imagine asking for a spinal or an epidural procedure while in labor. It would be so hard to hold still and with such a potentially bad outcome should the mother move during the procedure due to a contraction!

Who would choose this voluntarily? I really wonder how anyone could choose a hospital birth more than once. Who would volunteer for an epidural or a spinal? How could you subject yourself to this torture again?

When I gave my brother a kidney, some years before we had children, the worst part for me was surrendering myself to the doctor's care — their needles, blood tests, and knives. I hated entrusting my life to the hands of the hospital personnel. So when our neighbors, Pam and Gerry tried home birth years before we had children I remember feeling a kinship with Pam in her hatred of hospitals and needles. We also saw their level of comfort with the idea of home birth and their certainty that they had chosen the best of the alternatives. They seemed at peace with their decision. So when our time came to have children we did the reading to substantiate home birth.

Unfortunately for our neighbors, their first baby was also in an impossible position for birth. After many hours of labor at home and in the hospital they had a c-section delivery. I thought later, that Pam must be nuts to try a home birth again with her second child after having a c-section with the first. Why not just have another c-section and get the job done? But I realized later I just didn't know what it was like to have this surgery. After my own c-section delivery I knew why she didn't want another one and was willing to give home birth another try. In fact, we joked that maybe there was something about our street that was causing these home birth babies to wind up as c-section deliveries. Pam's second baby also added to the 3% c-section rate at Homefirst, the only repeat c-section Homefirst had experienced to date. So when Maura was born at home Pam was so thrilled that she wrote a poem to her on the occasion of Maura breaking "the c-section curse" on Talman Avenue.

Home Birth
to Maura with Love

I washed your blanket
in Woolite
the morning
you began
pushing your way to life.
Not knowing what else to do
I paced like a 1950's Dad.
Dried your blanket
twice
up and down
up and down
the stairs
its thick cotton trim
stubbornly
staying damp.
You stubbornly
clinging to
your first home.

Dry at last!
I delivered

your blanket
with trepidation
down the street
of home births gone awry-
My own Elizabeth and
Annie,
and your own brother, Patrick,
all choosing
in the final stages
to be lifted into life
by skilled surgeon hands
not the hands of home.

"Mom's at eight," they said
at the front door.
"Want to say hello?"
I climbed the stairs
with reverence reserved for Sunday
and saw your mother, looking fine
breathing deeply
from the king size bed.
Between contractions
telling tales of life
on Talman Avenue
to the midwife
in the rocker.
I pointed out the handy velcro closure
on your hooded newborn wrap.
Could hardly wait
to behold you wiggling inside the
flannel folds.

Section Two: Home Birth Stories

I hugged your Mom and Dad,
 told them
I knew they could do it,
that you would break
the c-section spell this time.
Leaving their house
in that electric moment
I knew there was nothing else
to do
but simmer
an evening meal
slowly, in great suspense
for this
transitional team.
Surely you'd be here by sundown!

Dinner was well over-done by nine.
We worried.
Maybe the hospital
had called out to you too?

Till the phone call came
to end this long day.
"It's a baby!"
"It's a girl!"
your tired Dad
announced.
"She's beautiful!
Looks just like her brother did.
Don't know how she'll feel
about that in a few years."

We danced in the kitchen at our
house.
Squealing the news to each other.
I exhaled relief
as if it were my own perfect baby.
Inhaled the happiness.
It's a girl!
Born at home
March 15th
Blessing our street.
Wrapped in a clean
new blanket.

by Pam Bradley
May 1, 1994

So Much Better

Home birth was so much better than I ever thought
it could be. It was really wonderful. I know that I will
not persuade any of my siblings to have a home birth,
however, among the family's 27 cousins some of my
nieces have seen those horrible birth movies shown in
their high school biology classes. They have seen the
needles and knives and stirrups in the movies, but they
have also seen what I chose. It would be so nice if young
people could not only learn about how a baby gets into
this world but learn also about home birth as an alter-

native way; that birth can happen without the mother being strapped down, without IVs, drugs and episiotomies.

Birth can happen by going about your day, respecting what your body is doing. All this has been going on for thousands of years and most of us can get there too!

Section Three

History of Home Birth in Chicago

History of Home Birth Chicago Style

8

*It is dangerous to be right
on a subject which
the established authorities
are wrong.*
— Voltaire

Looking back a hundred years

Dr. Joseph B. DeLee, "He always waits for the baby" Time *magazine cover story May 25, 1936*

Obstetrics was barely a specialty in 1895, when Chicago's own Dr. Joseph Boliver DeLee took an interest in it. Mortality rate was high for mothers and babies, especially for the impoverished mothers of the city. DeLee became the expert at delivering babies and was generally rated the best obstetrician in the United States. In his career he delivered around 8,000 babies himself and supervised the safe delivery of 100,000 more.

Section Three: History of Home Birth in Chicago

In 1895, Dr. DeLee opened a dispensary on Maxwell Street to deliver women of the city of Chicago in their own homes. *Time* magazine said,

> He was abysmally poor at the time and only four years out of Chicago Medical College. Chicago Jews gave him $500.00. A Christian doctor gave him a stove, a table, some chairs and an old carpet. His family supplied linens. From a second-hand store he got two beds. With that he started Chicago's first maternity dispensary in a $12.00 a month flat in a Ghetto tenement.

"On one occasion 13 cents and half a loaf of stale bread represented the floating assets of the institution. I went home and borrowed $10 from my father," said DeLee of those hard times.

At first he had no patients at all because he was renting a fourth floor walk-up and pregnant women didn't want to climb up there. Then when he got a first floor, cold water flat and hung a sign "Free Delivery Care", still no one came because the mothers were used to being delivered by neighborhood untrained midwives, not doctors, so they were skeptical. He had to go door to door canvassing till he attracted a handful of patients. He had to convince the mothers that birth was safer with a doctor, there was less death and his services were free.

"He was a convincing man," Dr. Beatrice Tucker, later his assistant, said of DeLee. For ten years he worked "schnoring", a Yiddish expression, begging for

186

money to build a hospital. He was often treated horribly, once even thrown down the stairs. He actually wrote DeLee's Obstetrics while potential donors kept him waiting in their offices for three or four hours before they would see him.

DeLee was convinced by this time, that the only way to teach medical staff how to deliver babies was to have them do it under his watchful eye. But he needed a teaching hospital of his own to work from. He knew how to use the forceps and he knew how to prevent childbed fever. Dr. DeLee knew how to prevent crisis with good prenatal care, sterile techniques and by watching the mother throughout labor. DeLee wanted to share this information with other doctors in the name of making birth safe for the city's poor. At the time more women were dying of childbirth than of cancer. Childbed fever killed one in four hundred women.

"He made a good appearance. He was a very handsome man, six feet tall, thin. When I met him in 1929 he was about fifty years old and had white hair, pretty hair, a white mustache and white goatee. He wore nothing but white in the Hospital. White morning coat, white starched collars, white-wash ties, white shirt and stiff white cuffs. Meticulously groomed." Dr. Tucker said of him in, *Maxwell Street, Survival in a Bazaar*, a book by Ira Berkow, which recounts the lives of famous Chicagoans of this area.

From the meager beginnings of the dispensary his reputation grew. Doctors, residents, interns, medical students and nurses went on deliveries with DeLee to see first hand how babies could be safely delivered under any condition which might arise. Some of Dr. DeLee's beliefs regarding birth were that "the increasing tendency to perform c-section deliveries was to be condemned," and that "the lack of prenatal care is responsible for many deaths." These prophetic words were spoken in 1936 when he was being honored by *Time* magazine as their feature story and cover photo.

In following years DeLee did manage to raise the funds to build two Lying-In Hospitals — the first on 51st Street, later sold to Provident Hospital, and then the Chicago Lying-In Hospital in 1929, affiliated with University of Chicago. Dr. Beatrice Tucker was hired as a resident at Chicago Lying-in Hospital in 1929 while DeLee was out of town because "he didn't believe in women doctors. He was not happy when he returned to work to find the first woman resident there. But he got over it." Tucker recalled. DeLee and Tucker, as it turned out, ran the Chicago Maternity Center for over 40 years.

In 1932, the University of Chicago Hospital released their dispensary to Dr. DeLee and its name became the Chicago Maternity Center, where he and his staff continued to deliver 3,600 babies a year primarily to the poor of Chicago and to teach over 400 medical students a year from four Chicago area schools and physicians from all over the U. S. and abroad. Those first three years DeLee financed the Center himself, relying on students and residents for help. During his time Dr. DeLee taught obstetrics to more that 3,500 nurses, 7,000 medical students and 540 postgraduate doctors. He did become an internationally respected obstetrician whose goals were to teach medical personnel safe delivery of infants and to provide prenatal care and safe home births for the city's indigents outside of Cook County Hospital which was vastly overcrowded.

Dr DeLee organized and worked with the board of directors till his death in 1941. He was saluted on his October 28 birthday one year by the Mother's Aid Club with their song composed to the tune of "The man of the Flying Trapeze."

"There once was a doctor whose name was DeLee
Best of obstetrical doctors was he.
Expensive for rich, for the poor he was free,
This wonderful Dr. DeLee."

— Dr. Beatrice Edna Tucker, Director of Chicago Maternity Center, 1932-1973

"For nearly 80 years, The Chicago Maternity Center, formerly the Maxwell Street Dispensary, specialized in delivering babies at home," reported Jim Bowman in a *Chicago Tribune Magazine* article of 1979.

"Dr. Beatrice Tucker and her assistant, Dr. Harry Benaron, along with 10 or so resident physicians and an equal number of medical students and nurses lived like firefighters — always ready to respond to a call," the article elaborated.

Students from several Chicago medical schools were required to do a rotation with Dr. Tucker at the Maxwell and Newberry Street location. For 40 years Dr. Tucker, distinguished 1922 graduate of Rush Medical School, first woman intern ever appointed to Evanston Hospital, and first woman resident of the University of Chicago

Lying-In Hospital, taught young doctors how to deliver babies. Hers was the only home delivery service for pregnant women in the country staffed by physicians. "When they came over to the maternity center," recalled Helen Hoffman, then executive director of the Center, "they'd live here and they didn't have much time off."

In his book, *Maxwell Street, Survival in a Bazaar,* Ira Berkow wrote of Dr. Tucker's living arrangement at the Center, "In her basement boudoir Tucker was blown upon by grime from what's as filthy a street corner as you'll find in our so-called civilized world. Sleeping a couple of hours in the gray of morning after a night of birth helping, she'd be roused by bawling hawkers and a terrific quacking of doomed ducks of the Maxwell Street Market."

During Dr. Tucker's years at the Center, it was estimated that she and her staff delivered as many as 100,000 babies from 1932 until 1973. "We had a respectably low infant mortality rate," said Dr. Tucker modestly. The truth was that the Chicago Maternity Center had the lowest infant and maternal death rate in the nation, despite the fact that the staff was delivering some of the nation's poorest patients, many with no prenatal care, who notified the Center at the last minute when birth was imminent. From 1932 to 1937, during its first five years as a center separate from the Chicago Lying-in Hospital, only 12 of the 14,000 women it cared for died from obstetric causes — fewer than one per 1,200 deliveries. At that time the national average was one maternal death per 175 deliveries. The Chicago Maternity Center's infant death rate of 3 per cent was half of the national rate. Dr. Tucker explained to Paul de Kruif in his 1938 book, *The Fight for Life*, the secret of the Center's low death rate. "We sit and wait." She also elaborated for de Kruif that childbirth "must march to its outcome with the very least possible scientific meddling."

Never Turned Down a Case

"Dr. DeLee," (founder of the Center and Dr. Tucker's mentor), "told me never to turn a case down, just do the best I could," explained Dr. Tucker in a 1979 *Chicago Tribune* article about her work. "We went to anybody who called," she said. "All the family had to provide was a stack of newspapers. We brought the rest. It didn't cost the family much to have a baby at home. We'd merely sterilize our instruments on the kitchen stove."

In an attempt to keep down infection and bring the standards of the hospital to the home it was standard procedure to deliver the babies on the family's kitchen table, covered by newspaper, with Dr. Tucker and her staff wearing masks and hair coverings. However, there were times when patients called Dr. Tucker's office too late in the labor for her to prepare her hospital-like setting for birth at home. Dr. Tucker and her staff were sometimes called to frightened households in the night where a birth, unattended by medical staff, had resulted in a baby half born with the shoulders unable to deliver or where a mother would have hemorrhaged to death if it were not for the skill and quick action of Dr. Tucker.

"Oh, I saw everything under the sun down there on

Section Three: History of Home Birth in Chicago

Maxwell Street. I delivered babies in alleys, on dirt floors, by candlelight, by a heated iron stove, crawling into attics," she recalled in *Maxwell Street*. In one emergency birth situation she was even forced to ax through a door to get to a wider front stairway in order for the ambulance staff to carry a woman down and off to the hospital.

By 1973 the political scene had changed at Chicago's teaching hospitals. Plans were underway to build the 18 million dollar Prentiss Women's Hospital as part of Northwestern University. By this time many of the ladies who had done fundraising on the Chicago Maternity Center's board were replaced by their husbands and their husbands' friends, corporate executives in health related industries. It was felt at the time, that these husbands, due to their industrial positions, could do an even better job of raising funds for the Center than their wives had done. Soon these prestigious members of the fundraising board of the Chicago Maternity Center were also invited to join the board of the developing Prentiss Women's Hospital.

It has been strongly stated in a 1976 Kartemqiun film, *The Chicago Maternity Center Story*, that it was in the interest of these executives to build another hospital which would consume the goods their local companies produced. "Today there are more profits in health care than in the steel, auto, and defense industries...The Chicago Maternity Center was outdated, delivering babies, not profits," the film commentator states.

Northwestern Hospital had promised that the Chicago Maternity Center would be able to continue its

192

equal care for all and its home birth services as part of the new Prentiss Women's Hospital. However, after the funds rolled in, due in a large part to the good reputation and fundraising abilities of the Chicago Maternity Center, support by Northwestern Hospital was withdrawn.

Chicago Maternity Center Closes Its Doors

By 1974, despite protest from the women of the Center and WATCH (Women Acting to Control Health Care), Northwestern Hospital administrators now wanted all patients to deliver their infants in the hospital, not at home. They would now train their own doctors in birthing procedures without Dr. Tucker's assistance, and this training did not include a belief in the option of home birth. This kind of policy forced the closing of Chicago Maternity Center.

"I felt badly about the center closing," Dr. Tucker told the *Chicago Tribune* in 1979. "I really believed in the work we were doing." Dr. Tucker continued in private practice after the closing of the Center, "but by 1975 I had 20 babies to deliver in one month. It was too much." (She was 78 years old at the time.) It was at this point in her career that she met Dr. Mayer Eisenstein.

Suzie, Dr. Tucker's Former Daughter-in-law, on Dr. Beatrice Tucker

Suzie: Dr. Tucker was quite a woman and really a great mother-in-law. When she decided to adopt her first baby she was single and about 48 years old. She had a broken leg from a car accident when they first brought the baby to her. She was the first single woman in Illinois to ever adopt a baby. Three years later she adopted another son. Her energy was boundless. With her busy work schedule she had to hire a live-in nanny for the boys so that they would be well cared for during her irregular and unpredictable working hours. The nanny became a well-loved family addition.

Dr. Tucker was a driven worker. She worked all the time. Even late in her life she tried to retire, but that lasted only about four months. She needed to work. So she came back to Chicago very soon after her Florida retirement and went to work for a clinic in the Pilsen community.

I remember that she thought it somewhat odd that she developed a following of "hippies" who worked to help keep the Chicago Maternity Center open in the 1970s. She was their hero. They assumed she embodied their politics. However, I believe she just wanted every-one, especially poor people, to have safe, affordable births of their children.

Dr. Tucker Delivers Her Grandchild

At the time of my first pregnancy I was married to Dr. Tucker's oldest son. With Dr. Beatrice Tucker as my mother-in -law it never occurred to me to have a baby in the hospital. My step-mother had had my step-sister at home through the Chicago Maternity Center and my aunt, Edith Abear, had had her children at home. She later became one of the founders of La Leche League. So, I was comfortable with the home birth concept.

When my first baby was due I, of course, began labor at home. However, Fatima was a large baby (8 lb. 11 oz) and her head was not in a position to deliver. She was in the birth canal but not able to move all the way down when we transferred to Northwestern Hospital, where we met Dr. Tucker's assistant, Dr. Harry Benarin and about twenty medical students.

I remember them asking me if I could get into this position and that position. I told them, "No I can't get into these positions. I have a baby stuck down there!" All these medical people were gathered around me because they were going to get to see the delivery of a baby using the DeLee forceps. It was 1974 and they got me all fixed up with a saddle block. Then they pushed the baby back up into the birth canal and manually turned her the right way. I was told to breathe and mimic pushing. I couldn't feel an urge to really push due to the saddle block. But it worked, she delivered on her own. When they brought her to me I remember asking if she would always look as she did then, with a cone shaped head.

After the birth the hospital staff wouldn't even let me touch my baby because I had a fever of 99 degrees. Of course, I had a fever, I told them. I had just had a saddle block. They were giving her formula in the hospital nursery and I was only allowed to see her through the window. I marched back to my room and chugged down a whole pitcher of ice water so that when they checked my temperature again it was normal. Only then

195

did I get to hold my own baby.

I had no idea that the hospital would be such a bad experience. I hadn't chosen home birth, as some women had, based on a previous bad hospital experience. I had an open mind about hospitals but had wanted a home birth based on my mother-in-law's ability to deliver our child at home. I discovered, after my first hand experience, that I didn't want to go back there for birth ever again.

Dr. Tucker and Dr. Eisenstein — the Past and Future

When our second child was born Dr. Eisenstein wasn't very much older than I was. He attended our birth with Dr. Tucker because she was getting up in years and didn't want to deliver her own grandchild by herself this time. Dr. Eisenstein was a new doctor and so laid back. Dr. Tucker was so much more the sterilizing hospital type. Of course both of them treated their patients very well, it was just different. I'd say that Dr. Tucker brought forward the best of the past and Dr. Eisenstein was able to pick up on that and expand it into his own style. Dr. Tucker was from a time when babies were born at home all the time. She was able to teach the new Dr. Eisenstein that birth takes time to happen, but that it can happen at home safely and without risk.

Dr. Eisenstein was the young natural birth advocate, in favor of giving the mother more of a lead and using less intervention such as episiotomies or iv's. He certainly developed this style further over the years and

196

developed an emphasis on breastfeeding which wasn't too popular at the time. I remember, with my first baby, I was told by the pediatrician to nurse only fifteen minutes on each side every two hours.

With our second child, I was encouraged by Dr. Eisenstein to attend La Leche League where they believed in nursing on demand. People were generally horrified then about nursing in public and about home birth. You can tell in all our family photos that I took breastfeeding to heart. Over 23 years now I have had six little children in my life (all born at home with the Homefirst staff except the first one I mentioned earlier.) I am nursing a baby in all our twenty three years of family photos. My children were nursed in chronological order for 9 months, then 2 years, then 14 months, 2 years, 2 years and with the last one, at age four, there is still a thirty second nurse before bed time. The importance of nursing was really stressed in the Homefirst practice!

These were the developments that grew at Homefirst, there was a concentration on breastfeeding and on the mother and her comfort. I'd say that Dr. Eisenstein really built up the strength in his practice that the best source of information in labor is gained by listening to the mother. He was always a strong advocate for the mother.

My own first born will be having her second baby with Homefirst. She has a great relationship with one of the Homefirst doctors and loves his laid back attitude about birth. She and her husband are both very pleased with the care he has given them and so we are beginning another generation of home birth babies within our family.

A Teen Daughter's Perspective

Suzie's teenage daughter, Abear, came home during her interview and offered a teen's perspective on the birth of her brothers and sister at home.

Abear: At home I remember just watching the babies come out. It wasn't a big scary deal. I was around for the last three births. It isn't anything like the health class birth movie they show in high school! The movie was so terrifying. It was the grossest thing! In the movie the women looked like they were so out of it. They were not feeling anything. They had pain killers and forceps for their births. The doctors were pulling on the babies heads. It was so sick!

Suzie: When you see the real thing there is something so special in the air. Everyone gets so caught up in the event when that baby starts to come! It is nothing like the movies!

Section Four

The Founding of La Leche League

Beginnings of
La Leche League

What is best for the baby
is best for the whole family
— Marian Tompson

Marian Tompson, one of the founders of
La Leche League International

"When I was in high school I read a Ladies Home Journal article about a Doctor Grantly Dick-Reed and the idea of natural childbirth. It stuck in my head for some reason. When I was pregnant years later I went to Marshall Field's Store and asked if they had a book authored by this doctor. I had remembered his name all those years! I bought *Childbirth Without Fear* (last updated 5th edition, 1987) that day. I read it and believed everything I read.

Fortunately for me, I did find a doctor who would go

along with my wishes to try a natural, drug-free delivery in the hospital. Bless his heart, he honored our agreement unlike many other doctors who would agree to a natural birth but then insist that you needed intervention when the time came.

I Was the Only One Awake

When I actually went to the hospital to have my first child the staff acted as if I were there to have my leg amputated that day. No one even mentioned what a special day it must be for me. I was the only one on the delivery floor awake in labor. All the other mothers were "knocked out" till after their births. They threw a sheet over my head and, as if I weren't even there, the doctors in the labor room talked amongst themselves about their dates and their dreams. No one even talked to me.

My hospital room was next to the delivery room that day. My husband was told he couldn't stay with me if there was someone in the delivery room. Of course, there were women coming and going from the delivery room so they sent my husband home. He drove home and said to himself, "What am I doing here?" and turned around to come back to the hospital.

While he was gone a nurse walked in and said, "We have to put out the lights now. It's night. Time to go to sleep!" So, there I was — having contractions, in the dark, alone, in a strange place with a sheet over my head! It seems so cruel now to think of it. But, you know, they didn't really know at that time that what they were doing was so bizarre.

202

While my husband was driving back and forth from home to the hospital my own doctor checked on me and said, "Whatever you are feeling right now, if you feel like you can stand this, then you can do it. It won't get any harder than this." That was all he had to say. I completely relaxed, feeling that if he said it, he must know!

I had to do a lot of pushing with a posterior positioned baby. When the doctor suggested using the forceps to make things much faster I remembered reading that for some reason forceps were a bad idea. So I told him I didn't want forceps. Melanie did eventually come out without help and it was like a miracle. All I saw was what looked like a doll and then she took a breath and it was a live person!

Soon after her birth a nurse gave me a shot to prevent excessive bleeding. I guess they didn't know that all you have to do to prevent excessive bleeding is nurse your baby. I reacted to the shot with an "ouch!" and the nurse exclaimed, " Oh, I thought you couldn't feel anything!" I hadn't been yelling and screaming so she figured I must not be feeling any pain. (I had overheard another doctor in the delivery room telling a woman if she didn't shut up he'd walk out and leave her alone.) Can you imagine?

After our first birth my husband became very smart. He wouldn't let anyone relate to me their wild or frightening tales of childbirth. It was his protective attitude along with the support I got from the book by Doctor Reed that made all the difference for me. I felt protected. Nowadays, for women, the high-tech procedures used prenatally, can be so frightening (and so inaccurate, all too often.)

What I wanted from then on was to have a baby at home but it wasn't until I was expecting my fourth baby that I discovered Doctor Gregory White. He lived in the same town and went to the same church as I did. And he delivered babies at home. I was delighted. My husband wasn't so sure, wanting, of course, to have the safest delivery possible. Being an engineer, he was coming from a different point of view.

There was a great study from Chicago Lying-In Hospital which my husband had read. They had delivered babies at home, on kitchen tables, to women with no prenatal care. Their home birth statistics were better than any others (home or hospital) for safety. That was all he needed to be convinced of the safety of home birth. I heard him on the phone after we had our first home birth. He said, "You know, the doctor didn't even have to be here!" He was so amazed at how simple birth was compared to what his delusions had been.

Home Has A Special Meaning

To my great surprise and joy my first daughter to become pregnant wanted to come home to my home to have her baby. She said, "We are living in a rented place which has no special meaning. But home would have a special meaning." So this started a tradition among our daughters to come to my house for their deliveries. I missed only one home birth due to a conference I was attending. By the time I got someone to speak for me at my sessions I arrived home too late. But that granddaughter loves me anyway. There have been nine grand-children born at home and three born at the hospital due to transfers in labor. But these babies, including a set of twins, were all natural deliveries. Dr. Eisenstein was present for the birth of my first grandchildren, the twins Nathan and Benjamin.

I never insisted that I be present at the births. I wanted what would be the most comfortable for my daughters and my sons-in-law. They all knew I'd support their wishes whatever they were. One son-in-law wasn't so sure about having me around. He felt I was the expert and he might do something wrong. But , I've found that by the time the mothers are in transition the fathers all want you to stay in the room because they really don't know what is happening and they appreciate the reassurance.

One son-in-law watched his baby come out and saw that the head looked blue. He was afraid that something was wrong or even that the baby was dead. But those of us standing at the foot of the bed were all smiling so he knew it must be all right. My daughter in labor also said, "Just by looking at the smiles on your faces I knew everything was okay."

An Unexpected Joy

This has been such an added joy to my life that I never expected. But this is what the next generation has wanted! Even though it has meant coming home under all different circumstances. One daughter and her husband drove up from Champaign, Illinois as soon as labor started. One daughter flew in from the northeast in her husband's cargo plane, strapped in a little jump seat, one month before the birth. It was easy for me, I was already at home! But they were willing to do what it took to make it home for the births.

All my daughters have nursed their babies. I never said a word about it to them. They knew that if they strongly objected it would be okay with me, but they grew up surrounded by La Leche League; one daughter even edited the League's newsletter. They all put together manuals and folded and stapled literature at home. And they have all felt so sorry for any babies not breast-fed.

A Revelation

"Mary White, wife of Dr. Gregory White, and I were talking at our church picnic one summer. By this time I had had four babies and Mary had had six. Mary had experienced a few problems nursing her first child even though her husband was a doctor. Some of the other women at the picnic were talking with us about similar problems they had with nursing that prevented them from continuing. Mary and I noted that these were the same problems we had had. This was a revelation. We thought we were the only ones who had difficulties with nursing. The other women had believed their doctors, who had told them such inaccurate things as, "You won't have enough milk," or "You must supplement with formula." These statements and others like them had stopped them from nursing altogether.

It seemed to me that it wasn't fair that women who wanted to do the very best thing for their babies couldn't get any help with nursing. So we decided to get together with our friends, who were pregnant or nursing, to share experiences. I'd take my children and walk over to Mary's house and we'd talk.

One day as I stood on the doorstep to leave Mary's house we were in the midst of deciding if we had enough time to lead these local meetings for our friends. We had ten children between us to take care of! I remember saying, "You know, Mary, if we are going to be helping mothers and babies, we'll be helping families and if we are helping families then we are helping society. So let's give it a try."

Let's Give It a Try

They made me president of this endeavor because they said it was my idea. Betty Wagner was made treasurer because she had once worked in a bank. Edwina Froehlich was secretary. We sat with our friends and discussed the only two things we knew about in print on the subject of breastfeeding. One was a *Readers Digest* article, "Breast is Best", and the other a pro breastfeeding article by a Dr. Richardson, a physician who was all for nursing. His perspective was a mechanical, scientific one, however. I remember he said that if the baby wasn't nursing enough give the baby an enema. He must have felt that if you took something out then more could go in. But he was supportive of breastfeeding being the best, so we read his article too.

207

Section Four: The Founding of La Leche League

We read these articles and talked about them at first. Then we got more organized with four meeting topics and a fifth meeting for fathers. We recognized then that fathers had to be supportive for nursing to work. Doctors White and Ratner, home birth colleagues, would run the meetings for the men. In those days the men had to meet separately. It wouldn't have been acceptable to meet together. We couldn't even use terms like "nipple" or "breast" in mixed company. We became known as La Leche League because we couldn't even run a newspaper ad with the mention of breastfeeding support group in those days.

My husband would drive around and pick up the other fathers. There wasn't so much television then to interfere with your evening plans so if Tom Tompson was coming to pick you up — you went. They would meet at one house and usually have beer with the breastfeeding talk. They loved these new concepts that included real roles for fathers. No one had given them an opportunity before this to comment or ask questions. So these lively meetings would go on until midnight sometimes. These were very popular meetings.

Beyond Franklin Park

We never imagined that things would grow beyond Franklin Park, but soon, due to word of mouth, there were two new groups forming. People would come to our meetings that we didn't even know. I remember one woman came who wasn't nursing a baby. Finally I asked her why she came. She said, "You women seem to like

208

having children and you like your children so much that I thought if I hung around some would rub off on me."

I first met Dr. Eisenstein around this time when he was a young medical student learning from Dr. Robert Mendelsohn. Dr. Mendelsohn would send his students to our La Leche League office to talk with us about breastfeeding, a topic not very well covered in medical school, but one important to Dr. Mendelsohn, a leading children's pediatrician at the time. Mayer was so lucky to have Dr. Mendelsohn for a mentor in med school. But in a way it must have made medical school even harder for him. Mayer would stand up for what he believed, even if it meant disagreeing with his professors. Issues such as the importance of breastfeeding or the dangers of inoculations would not make you very popular in medical school.

With the help of Dr. Herbert Ratner, author of *Child Family Digest* , and a mentor of Dr. Eisenstein's, we discovered that we weren't simply teaching breastfeeding, but mothering through breastfeeding. It was different in so many ways from the mothering of bottle fed babies. The nursing babies were in bed with their parents, they had no feeding schedules, the infants went everywhere with their mothers and parents didn't have sitters for the nursing infants. It was so different that sometimes we wondered how to do all this! Support for this type of mothering was the basis of La Leche League from the beginning. Now, forty years later, the League members are still discussing these same topics and more, holding meetings in 66 countries with 32,000 leaders trained to run the meetings.

Section Four: The Founding of La Leche League

The older I get the more important I feel the work of the League is. I can see the ripple effect in so many families, the changes in the perceptions of parenthood on the part of those in La Leche League. The courage these families have to step out and defy the way things are usually done in a community! This takes a lot of courage.

I will always be in La Leche League. It is changing the world into a world that becomes sensitive to what babies, children, we, ourselves, all need. An infant's beginning is so important that if we do it right we don't have to waste energy later on trying to fix up what was handled wrong at the beginning.

La Leche League has put me in touch with the most wonderful people in the world — people who care about other people, people committed to doing the best for their children.

I believe that if we had all gotten what we really needed from the start, we'd be the best people we could be, doing what we came here to earth to do. That's what we do for our children when we feed them right, from the start.

It is to Doctor Eisenstein's credit that he presents breast-feeding in such a way that all the mothers in his Homefirst practice want to nurse their infants. I'm sure he has done a lot of good for the world by helping so many people get a good start with breast- feeding. I'll never discount the value of the birth experience; however, I'm sure Dr. Eisenstein would agree that breast-feeding over a period of time helps the infant in the adjustment to the outside world. It also helps the parents in

210

knowing themselves and who they are in relationship to the infant. This is extremely important."

An interview with Viola Lennon, one of the founders of Le Lache League and her daughter Elizabeth Lennon

"The first three of my 10 children were born in the hospital before I decided I'd never go back there again for a birth. It was right after I delivered my third child, Mimi, that I woke up coughing and miserable with a real ace cold. The nurses wouldn't bring in the new baby for me to breast-feed because they thought she would get my cold.

That was where it all started!

'I want that baby immediately!' I demanded.

There was no "rooming in" for the newborns in those days. They were kept in the hospital nursery and brought to the mothers once every four hours for a feeding. However, my doctor had always gotten around this rule for the Lennon babies. He ordered that my infants be brought to me every two hours. This was smart because by the time I nursed and burped them it was almost time for them to be brought back to me again. The nurses would gripe about it and tell me they never heard of such a thing. But it was a smart way around the ridiculous four hour feeding schedules that were so popular then. But they weren't going to bring me this baby at all since I had a bad cold.

So I told them I'd have to call my husband's legal firm if she was not brought to me. I knew it was very important to get nursing established with the baby in those early days and this delay was not acceptable. Your emotions are at the surface of your skin after a birth. I decided then that I'd never go back to the hospital to have a baby. By the way, they did bring her to me and she never caught my cold.

A New Term — "Mothering"

It was after Mimi's birth that I was invited by my friend, Edwina, to a meeting about breast-feeding and mothering. I had been very successful at breast-feeding, inspired by Edwina who had nursed her children. By this time breast-feeding to me just seemed the natural thing to do but I was interested in the idea of "mothering." It was a new term for me. I didn't know the others at the meeting but as things happened, all of us at that meeting turned out to be the founders of La Leche League.

We realized at our meetings that by nursing our babies we had to stand up for things not currently popular in our culture. It was a time of more severe disciplining of children and of adherence to a four hour feeding schedule for new babies. At the time lots of women said of breast-feeding, "I'm too nervous to nurse a baby," or "I won't have enough milk." My own friends admired me for nursing but said they surely couldn't. Breast-feeding wasn't 'modern' in the 50's. The bottle fed baby could be passed around for anyone to feed. Mothers felt freed up by bottles.

Those are actually the same kinds of things people

still say today. I have heard my own daughters in the 90s still being asked, "Didn't you just feed that baby?" after someone would see the new mother nursing a fussy baby for comfort soon after it had been nursed for hunger. That is such a threat to a new mother. I know I faced those types of remarks all the way through. These were the kinds of things we discussed at those early meetings.

Lots of the League meetings were held at my house. We had a large front room which could comfortably hold 20 people. It was not unusual for our house to be filled with nursing mothers, infants and toddlers. My own children were used to seeing League gatherings at our house. As a result of that exposure perhaps, all my daughters have nursed their babies and so have all my son's wives. My daughter who went to law school is so pro-breastfeeding that she is the most outspoken advocate at the League meetings.

I had my chance to be outspoken when my mother's friend's daughter, a Catholic nun and a nurse, brought a whole bunch of other nun nurses over from Taiwan years ago. The nuns were here to study within their field. One of the young nuns said on the topic of breast-feeding, "That was nice a long time ago." I piped up with, "breastfeeding is the Creator's gift to a new baby!" She had never thought of that!

Our First Home Birth

So I was in the League before I had my first home birth. Some of the other women in the group had had home births. They told me how relaxed they were at home. They said it was so nice that the doctor comes to you for the birth and the follow up visits after the birth. They said you could do as you pleased at home with no hospital procedures to follow.

Our first home birth was for our fourth child, Rebecca. It was in 1957 and home births were beginning to be heard of around Chicago. They were being done by Dr. Gregory White, who happened to be our doctor. He was the same doctor who cleverly helped us get around the four hour feeding schedules after our hospital births. At that time the biggest problem we anticipated was my own mother. We had tried to give her some hints that we were considering a home birth and she reacted with great opposition. I have always said that they must have knocked her out as she walked up the steps to the hospital to have her own babies. She had no recollection of any of her own labors and births, so she was very concerned about the idea of home birth.

We simply tried to keep it from her. The hardest part was making sure she didn't call or come over during the birth. We had invited my sister Pat to come over during labor. Of course my mother was trying to call Pat during that time and wondered why she wasn't answering. There we were trying to keep her away but, of course, after the baby was born she was quite positive about the whole thing and thereafter was always a very big help to me.

I enjoyed all my home births. I was so relaxed and comfortable at home. There were no complications for us. I never pushed more than three times and there was

214

a baby! One of the best parts of home birth for me is
that it affords mothers the opportunity to nurse right
away when the babies are more alert than they will be in
the next four days. It was really wonderful.

Nursing right away reminds me of one concern new
mothers in the Midwest have about their hospital delivered babies — the bilirubin count. Doctors scare so
many mothers about the jaundice their babies sometime
develop in the days after birth. (Studies show this seems
to be a concern on the part of Midwestern doctors but
not those on either coast.) If new mothers are simply
allowed to nurse their babies on demand the yellow col-
oring some of them develop doesn't become a problem. It
is a problem when the babies are taken away and given
water or formula. Water and formula will increase the
jaundice. As soon as the mother's milk supply comes in,
about the third day, the billirubin count goes down on
its own. If the mother has held and nursed her baby all
along, then nature handles the jaundice and there is no
problem.

Home is the Key Ingredient

Dr. White always told people who were fearful about
home birth just how fast a transfer to the hospital could
be made if necessary. Even those women in the hospital
who need c-sections generally have to wait about 45
minutes for the staff to prepare to do surgery on them.

I trusted Dr. White completely. I believe I could have
even had my twins at home with no problems; however,
Dr. White was on vacation at the time. They were born

in the hospital and turned out to be the simplest birth I had. Just because they were twins didn't automatically make it a complex delivery. It wasn't.

If I knew a family considering a home birth I'd review my own experiences for them. I'd tell them how relaxed and comfortable I was at home. Home is the key ingredient. I enjoyed it so much. I'd caution them too, that if their hospital labor extends over 24 hours in duration, then that is all the staff is willing to wait. Lots of women unfortunately miss 'the last act of their play." After all the labor and build up, the hospital will intervene with procedures which leave the mothers feeling like they missed the birth altogether. At home, you are allowed to labor as long as it takes so long as there aren't problems, of course.

My first born, Elizabeth, has delivered her two children at home with Dr. Eisenstein's practice. She has had a great influence on my family when it comes to delivering babies safely."

The following are Elizabeth Lennon's comments about home birth:

"When I was pregnant for the first time I started my prenatal visits with a high tech practice where the doctors talked natural birth, but "behind the curtain" was all the waiting machinery. But more about that later.

I wasn't going to automatically do just what my mother had done before me about birthing. But what convinced me ultimately to switch to a home birth practice was seeing my sister-in-law after she had a c-sec-

216

tion. She looked so awful that I was really scared. I knew my mom had looked fine at home after a birth — everyone looked fine at home — but my sister-in-law didn't.

My mother was convinced that something had gone wrong during the surgery.

Call Dr. Eisenstein

Mom said she was never so nervous. It took too long and my sister-in-law looked too sick afterwards. I saw her and said to myself, 'I better get more education!' Mom told me to call Dr. Eisenstein.

Other practices, including the one I had been with during this first pregnancy, give you an initial consultation where you are undressed, helpless on the table and for a fee! Dr. Eisenstein's consultation was free and just a talk first with both parents-to-be. I was so impressed that he just really wanted to consult. He wasn't trying to "sign us up." So, I was comfortable with this.

However, my husband, with a pre-med background from Northwestern, was more scared. He felt I had overstepped the limits this time. He had gone along with my feminism, keeping my own last name when we married, but not home birth! His friends, some still in med school, looked at us like we just told them we were going to perform brain surgery at home instead of have a baby at home. But bless his heart, David had come this far with me to the consultation, and he was willing to educate himself. Right away he liked Dr. Eisenstein, who said, 'You don't have to decide now.'

Section Four: The Founding of La Leche League

So we had time to educate ourselves. We did our reading. I was convinced that David would be all right if he read *The Home Court Advantage*, Dr. Eisenstein's own book on the subject of home birth. He did and then he was okay with it. I had the advantage of a subconscious memory that home birth was safe. But as the first born I had to investigate, to go around and come back to the idea myself.

It Doesn't Get Any Better Than That!

At my own first home birth my mother and sister were there with us. From the first twinges of labor to the birth was about 24 hours. Most of that time at home I was functioning pretty normally. We made a cake for the baby, went to lunch and took a walk. Things got serious for me only after midnight. We had been trying to watch a movie together but we all lost track of what was happening — especially me.

There were only about three hours of hard labor. Mom was so impressed by the assistance I received from the nurse who came to the house ahead of Homefirst's Doctor Dietz. Mom didn't have nurses at her home births and Susan was great, calm and helpful. I felt so blessed to have her there.

Pushing was brief and it was like magic when Jenna was born. We had champagne and the three of us were able to take this incredible nap together in the same bed. When we woke up mom came to make spaghetti for dinner. It doesn't get any better than that!

The next day my sister told an acquaintance who

was studying to be an ob-gyn that I had a baby yesterday and needed no stitches. This student wouldn't believe her!

My sister said, 'I should know. I was there!' She could tell by her face that she felt my sister must be mistaken especially since this was a first baby.

After a home birth you realize how undermining and arrogant the whole hospital thing is. For all those thousands of years how do they think we all got here? Mother Nature provides. She's much smarter than all those doctors at the hospitals. It's downright misogynistic. Even the female staff of the hospital is brainwashed. They wind up being harmful to new mothers too.

A Second Home Birth

With my second birth I had a case of sciatica. The baby's head and my sciatic nerve met about three weeks before the birth so I could hardly walk. Labor pains came one week before my due date so I wasn't sure this was real labor. But after only one hour the pains were ten minutes apart. We called Homefirst at that point. It was not even three hours into the process that the pains were serious. David didn't think the nurse or doctor would make it on time. So he called them back and Homefirst arranged to send out another nurse who was closer to us until the assigned nurse could get there.

Jude and Janita, nurses from Homefirst, were there and my mom and sister, Mimi. Mimi hung out with our older daughter and they made the new baby's cake together. Mimi came into the kitchen at one point to check on the cake in the oven and Mom said,'I think it will be another three minutes.' By this time Dr. Eisenstein was there and he replied, 'I think it will be longer than that!' He thought she meant the baby was coming and she was talking about the cake. I remember they all laughed and laughed about that.

By that time I wasn't laughing. I was in serious labor. It was a hard but uneventful labor. I remember lots of drinks and foot rubs. Our three year old, Jenna, wandered in and out to check on me that day in labor. It is amazing to me how mothers can look after their children even in labor. I remember holding her hand from time to time and telling her, "Mommy is okay. These are just the sounds women make when they are about to have a baby." Jenna never cried or got upset. There were people there for her and she moved in and out of the scene.

When the baby appeared so fast after such a short time Jenna was awestruck. You can tell by the wonderful look on her face in the photo when she first saw Tess. From then on she was really into being a sister and wanted to hold the baby.

I was so glad Tess was out and safe after such a short time. I think she would have come even faster if I had been more mobile. It was all amazing.

Highlights of My Life

My two home births were highlights of my life. We started from the first moments as a family. My husband saw the girls being born and he was there to hold them.

Our daughters have an incredible relationship because the older one was there to see her baby sister born.

I don't think you can persuade anyone to have a home birth. They have to be open to the idea already. But if someone were on the fence about it I'd encourage them to see Mayer Eisenstein for a consultation, to read *The Home Birth Advantage*, to talk to people who have had home births, to go to La Leche League meetings. Do comparison shopping as a consumer.

Section Five

Final Comments

The Last Word

OO VORCHARTA BACHAYIM
I have set before thee heaven and earth,
the life and the death.
I have set before thee the blessing and the curse.
Therefore,
Choose life.
— Deuteronomy 30:19

By Dr. Eisenstein and his Family

*I*t was at a Friday night birthday party for baby Jason, born on the previous Sunday, that the Eisenstein family had gathered with the baby's parents, Ingrid and Al. Dr. Eisenstein's oldest child, Jeremy, had been friends with Al since high school and both are now fathers. The influence of Dr. Eisenstein's work in their young lives had influenced not only Jeremy but also his good friend, Al, to choose home birth for their children. Both had married women who came to appreciate the choice of home birth and were gathered this night with their children; also Jeremy's sister Jennifer, and her children; Dr. Eisenstein and his wife, Karen, to welcome the latest home birth baby into the world with a cake and a gathering in the baby's honor. Each generation, each couple, each parent brought with them a perspective on home birth which they were willing to share as an addition to *The Home Birth Advantage.*

The evening's conversation went something like this:

Karen Eisenstein: Jennifer's birth in 1973 was my first home birth. After her brother Jeremy's hospital delivery two years before I knew that any other birth I might have would not be in a hospital. So, Jennifer's birth, my second delivery, was not simply my first home birth, it was an overcoming kind of experience. I overcame all the terrible things that had happened in the hospital when Jeremy was born. Of course, Jennifer's birth was much better than just an overcoming, it was great, but I did have to get over the hospital experience and it was her birth that did it. A comparison might be the example of a dog we used to have who did bad things. We now have the same kind of dog and I am waiting for him to do the same bad things, although he hasn't. As joyful as any home birth is, Jennifer's wasn't quite the same high as I got from all the others. I still had the fear I was carrying from the first birth. But Jennifer's delivery helped me to turn the corner on that fear.

Mayer Eisenstein: Dr. White always said that the mother has to overcome the first birth if she felt that the first birth was not all that it should have been. The second birth brings with it a letting go of the past experiences. The second birth is healing. That is certainly what Karen went through with Jennifer's birth.

Karen: Although I was at home, Jennifer's birth was done in a hospital mode. I spent most of the time in the bedroom. It was a very long labor and I was in that one room, in the bed. Mayer had not been delivering babies for very long at this time, so he didn't have the experience either that he later had at home births. So we acted as if we were in the hospital in the choices we made to stay put in one small space.

By contrast, yesterday was our third child's birthday. I was up in the morning yesterday at a time when I would have been in active labor with her 23 years ago. I e-mailed Alycia that hers was actually my first home birth. It was my first real home birth. It included everything I had seen and knew about home birth. I told Alycia that hers was my best birth. Mayer and I played backgammon during that labor. I was in the kitchen, the dining room, all over. It was very special. And so were all of the ones after that. They were all memorable and all awesome.

Mayer: I remember that after Alycia's birth I was supposed to wake up the other children. I ran in to get them but they were sleeping and wouldn't wake up! They were just so sleepy that they wouldn't get up till morning to see her.

Section Five: **Final Comments**

Karen: I knew that Jennifer's birth was the right thing. It was a million, trillion times better that the hospital birth I had had with Jeremy, but if you don't know how awesome awesome is, then good is really terrific. After the healing I did with Jennifer's birth, the rest of my children's births were awesome.

Mayer: This reminds me of our daughter-in-law, Susie, telling me that after Jennifer delivered her first child, she came over to see Jennifer. Susie was also pregnant with her first child. Jennifer told her how terribly hard all this had been. It had been a long and hard labor. But Jennifer was not very convincing because there she sat, nursing the new baby, looking fine. If someone had not seen the labor and delivery they would have said, "This is the easiest thing in the world. Look how wonderful the new mother looks!" With all those loving people around her it didn't look so hard.

Susie: (married to Jeremy): And after Jennifer's second child was born, I went to see her. When I got inside her apartment I said, "Where is Jennifer?" I actually didn't recognize her sitting on the couch because she looked so good. I remember Jennifer saying, "I'm right here!" And there she sat nursing the baby. She was dressed and looked so good.

Karen: At my last birth the kids all came home seconds after Zachary was born. They were all down the block until the birth. Jeremy, the oldest, walked in and cut the cord of his baby brother.

Mayer: This was the hardest job I ever had to coordinate. Karen wanted the other children there the second that baby was born. The kids were screaming in excitement and running down the street right after he was born. I had left the front door open for them to come in.

It is always so impressive to me that the overall feeling, after a home birth, is that this is just the way it is supposed to be, regardless of how hard the labor was. In a way this is a drawback to home birth. It looks so simple afterwards. In our age we look for sophisticated answers. But home birth is simple. It is not a rebellion against what we have learned about birthing over the centuries. But it can be viewed as a rebellion against unnecessary technological intervention which is so rarely necessary.

Al: When our baby was born a few days ago, it was just about an hour before Dr. Eisenstein's Sunday evening radio show. I was the first caller to the show. It must have looked like a setup with me saying, "We just had a baby!"

Karen: When Jeremy was learning to drive in high school, it was Al who was taking him out in the car, since Al was a little older than Jeremy. I was pregnant at the time with Zachary. It was Al who went out in the car with Jeremy to buy the things we wanted in order to have a party when Zachary was born. So, Al was around our house in the days that I was nursing babies and delivering the last one. He had plenty of experience with home birth at our house.

Al: I grew up in a house where we relied on our doctors for everything. We called the doctor whenever we were sick. After I met Jeremy I'd tell him I had medicine for this or that. He'd say, "Just give it a few days. That medicine will make it last longer!" The Eisensteins's advice was the complete opposite so after a while I just didn't take medicine anymore.

Mayer: I remember telling both Al and Jeremy that when they got married they didn't have the right to insist that their wives have home births; that their wives had the right to do what they wanted about the births of their children. However, both Al and Jeremy chose dynamic women who were most interested in what we had learned about birth. Both Susie and Ingrid were open to listening and making independent decisions about home birth. The same was true of Jennifer's husband, Dan. He was at our house visiting with Jeremy since they were about twelve years old. For him it was all second nature by the time he married Jeremy's sister, Jennifer.

Susie: When I was a couple of years old my mother remembered seeing Dr. Eisenstein on A.M. Chicago talking about home birth. I never had to convince my mom of anything. She loved the whole idea from the start.

I was the first person among my friends to have children. When I saw how good Jennifer looked after her delivery, I thought this was the way you were supposed to do it. But when I later saw my girlfriends having babies, how they looked and felt afterwards, I couldn't believe it! My mom and I walked into a hospital to visit my girlfriend and I didn't recognize her because she looked so bad. She was telling me about the episiotomy and how she couldn't walk, couldn't wear pants, she couldn't do anything.

I was walking the dogs the next day after I delivered

my daughter. I remember Mayer telling me it is not that you don't feel good but you should be careful not to over-do it. I was shopping in Marshall Field's store after three days!

Mayer: With Al and Ingrid I went over when the baby was one day old and Ingrid wanted to come over for a birthday party with us on Monday, the next day after the birth!

Ingrid:(married to Al): I really felt great even though this second birth was harder than the first for me. I was fine by Monday.

Susie: All my friends and Jennifer's friends think we're weird to have home births. But I knew that my husband and my father-in-law wanted the best for me, and home birth was it. I had two hours of active labor with my second child. I had just eaten a whole order of lasagna at the Rain Forest Cafe where we were celebrating a birthday and two hours later I had a baby!

Karen: Home birth is not something you can sell. Someone has to already be interested and then you can give them the information. You can only preach to the choir or someone who would like to join the choir.

Mayer: When Danielle was born, Susie's second child, it was the middle of the night and Karen and I later went home to bed. When we woke up the next morning we asked ourselves, "Did that really happen? Did Susie really have her baby or did we just dream it?"

Jennifer (the oldest Eisenstein daughter): However, both my births were awfully painful and long, in contrast to Susie's experience. But when it was over, it was over. I had my sisters and parents with me and I felt

231

great. But I don't have the expectation that the pain will be any less for me this next time. But when it is over I can forget about the pain. For this next delivery, in June, we will be living in our own house, for the first time. I can walk around, unlike before when everyone wanted me to walk the halls of our apartment building and I was so embarrassed to be in the hallway, in a robe, in labor.

Jeremy (the oldest Eisenstein son): For me the births of my own children feel similar to the births of my siblings. All the births feel like part of the same continuum.

Al: The people in my office talk about the births of their children, in hospitals. They talk about the experiences of c-sections, forceps deliveries and episiotomies.

When Josh, our first, was born they asked how it had gone. I said we had a home birth and had none of the usual stories. Everything was natural and went fine. Thank God, we didn't have any thing like their stories!

The men at work say their wives can't walk or go to the bathroom after a delivery. Oh, Man! I tell them I don't want to hear about it. After Jason was born a few days ago, I stopped in the office for a few hours, later in the week. I said it was great for the second time. They were all saying what credit they give my wife for doing this messy thing at home. They said their wives wouldn't want a messy house. But it wasn't really messy at all. It was fabulous.

My own brother asked me how I could not want to experience the high point of birth — the drive to the hospital. He recalled his 90 mile an hour race down the street when his child was born. He thought surely I'd want that memory too.

Ingrid: The first time we had a home birth I told no one because I didn't want to be asked if I was crazy. But the second time we told them and they were fine with it.

I felt so good the second time that I really could have gone in to work the next day.

Mayer: I have always been upset with people who say that I am just lucky in my practice. I never know what to say to that. I'd sure want to be affiliated with a "lucky" doctor whose practice has healthy babies and children with very few visits to the doctor for illness.

Susie: People have said to me that by having a home birth I missed a chance to go away for a while and have the hospital bring me food and handle the laundry. But I have to say that it was so nice to have my family helping me out and watching my other daughter. Kayla didn't have me gone for days and she was so welcoming of the new baby. No strangers were around opening the door to my room and asking me questions at odd times of the day and night. I had people who loved me, my own blanket and my own bathroom. Having a home birth was the best thing I have ever done.

Mayer: When I look around this room at my family and friends I am reminded of how babies are such gifts. They are one of the most enjoyable aspects of life. Siblings at a home birth always view the new baby as a natural part of the family, someone else who will soon be able to play. These are the good things, not problems, in life. Often we sell out for the material aspects of life instead.

Karen: Dr. Ratner always said that the greatest gift

you can give your child is Another sibling. He saw the
bigger picture. He was responsible for us having six
children because he dispelled the myth for us that children are a burden, a problem, a financial worry. He
taught us that the simplest things in life are the most
enjoyable; home birth, babies, family life, friends. And it
is a very special gift to be able to share what we have
learned with other familes.

A Sampling from the Radio Show
Family Health Forum

The following excerpts are from Family Health
Forum, a nationally syndicated radio call-in show hosted by Dr. Mayer Eisenstein It is a broadcast which aims
at keeping listeners informed on important health
issues affecting their families.

May 18, 1996
Doctor Eisenstein:

"As my first born granddaughter celebrated her first
birthday this week on May 16 I looked at one year old
Abby and said, "Thank you , G-d. We have been so
blessed."
My wife, Karen and our six children and now our
two grandchildren have all been blessed; blessed to have
been introduced to so many concepts that make for
strong and healthy families. We have been blessed to
know about home birth, breastfeeding and La Leche
League. We have been blessed to have as friends and

mentors the greatest home birth and pediatric health gurus of our times: Dr. Robert Mendelsohn, Dr. George Dietz, Dr. Beatrice Tucker, Dr. Herbert Ratner and Dr. Gregory White.

I am so blessed to work in my practice with such a wonderful staff: Doctors Peter Rosi, Mark Zumhagen, Paul Schattauer, Benjamin Lo , Elizabeth Baker and now also Penny Shelton-Hoffman, Jifunza Wright, Risha Raven and Jonathan Martinez and all the wonderful certified nurse midwives and registered nurses who work for Homefirst Health Services. I have learned so much from my staff both current and past as we have worked together in this wonderful profession which has enabled us to share in the beginnings of so many fabulous families.

I have been so blessed that my children and now grandchildren have had the influence of La Leche League in their lives, that they have all been nursed successfully through the marvelous input of this organization. Thank you, thank you, to all the nurses and doctors who have made it possible for us to have five of our children and our grandchildren born at home. I could have no greater pleasure as a father and grandfather than to know my family members have had these optimal spiritual and physical health experiences as infants, that of home birth and breastfeeding. There are no greater gifts from G-d or nature than these for the newborn.

I feel so blessed!"

Section Five: **Final Comments**

March 30, 1998

"As I see it there is one major reason to choose home birth for your family. It will change so many other aspects of your life for the positive and affect so many decisions that you make down the road. People who haven't chosen home birth have an easier time electing to have so many popular yet misguided medical procedures of the nineties performed on them and their family members: hysterectomies, by-pass surgeries, mastectomies, prostate surgeries, unnecessary antibiotics, even the surgical insertion of tubes in the ears of children with ear infections.

Today's doctors are performing too many unnecessary procedures which only lead to other unnecessary procedures. Those families born into hospital settings, feeding their infants bottles of cow's milk formula from the start are easy prey for doctors performing these surgeries and procedures. Any doctor who has successfully talked a family into a hospital birth or convinced them of the safety of infant formula has done that family great harm. This new family has been given an unhealthy start because they put their faith in a failing, misguided and unscientific system. However, they will most likely continue to entrust this medical model with the lives and health of their family members.

How can families protect themselves from this misguided medicine? Home birth and breastfeeding, home birth and breastfeeding, home birth and breastfeeding.

I can't say it enough. Parents choosing to give birth to their children at home and to feed their infants nature's most perfectly suited substance, mother's milk, have placed themselves in a different category from the start. They are people who question, question, question. Most doctors will not have answers to those questions because their unscientific methods are incorrect and even harmful.

No one can expect life values to come from doctors and health plans choosing to cover "death medicine", oriented around abortion, frequent mammograms, psa screenings. Doctors of this "death medicine" do not employ the scientific method. "Death medicine" insurance packages do not cover the most long term beneficial option for family health — home birth.

At Homefirst we have always aimed to support nature, to help nature do what it would have done on its own. So when we help nature it is not by providing drugs and surgery for the mother but by helping her walk around in labor, stay hydrated, fed and comfortable doing whatever it takes to help her give birth. Our doctors truly practice the ancient oath of Hippocrates, "Above all do no harm."

Once the baby is born nature is not helped by giving the infant cow's milk labeled "formula". Within our practice we do everything possible to help the new mother nurse her baby. We put her in touch with La Leche League leaders to answer her questions. We make sure that the nurses on our staff have been League leaders themselves. This is the way to have successful mothers.

And I guarantee that if you have a home birth and nurse your infant, you will later have trouble sending your children off for traditional institutional learning. You will have trouble agreeing to have them immunized.

Section Five: Final Comments

You will not be so quick to let a doctor cut off your breast or cut out your prostate. You will have trouble letting a doctor cut our your uterus.

Once that happens you will be moving yourself and your family into a healthy life style."

May 18,1996

"This week I read an article by Carl Rowan, editor of a syndicated column in the Chicago Sun Times, dated May 15, 1996. I really feel that Mr. Rowan doesn't know what he is talking about. Without knowing it, he is speaking from far left field on the topic of Express Delivery, the accepted term for mothers and babies leaving the hospital within 24 hours of the birth of their infants.

A bill introduced by Senator Bill Bradley of New York proposes to legislate a guarantee of hospital coverage for the mother and baby for 48 hours after a vaginal birth and 96 hours after a c-section delivery. I feel certain that the words "guarantee of hospital coverage" will in no time become "forced hospital stay." These legislators don't know what happens in hospitals!

President Clinton, on the air last week summarized the opinions of 100's of noted obstetricians, gynecologists, pediatricians and hospital administrators. They all concluded that no hospital can determine in 24 hours all the potential problems of babies who look normal at birth. Early release of infants can result in numerous problems with feeding, severe dehydration, brain damage and stroke.

I agree with Mr. Clinton. Early release can result in "problems with feeding, severe dehydration, brain damage and stroke." Why? Because these babies were born in the hospital. Their mothers received epidurals, electronic fetal monitoring, narcotic drugs, episiotomies, needles for hydration instead of oral hydration, forceps for deliveries, out of proportion numbers of c-section deliveries, separation of babies from their mothers, sugar water feedings and cow's milk formulas. Of course, this leads to damage! Why not keep them in hospitals all their lives! It will take that long to determine all the damage caused by the hospital stays in these periods of 48 or 96 hours!

U.S. legislators want to keep babies in the hospital longer than necessary; keep them in the hospitals of a country ranked 24th in the world as far as infant and maternal mortality; in a country where more babies are born in the hospital than any other country in the world. Our country endorses the two most damaging treatment plans ever devised by doctors: hospital birth and bottle feeding of new-borns. Our legislators want to guarantee these infants a stay in our hospital nurseries even longer than is currently favored by insurance companies.

Shame on them for not knowing their facts! Shame on President Clinton for wanting to be the champion of newborns but keep them in the hospital. I would be terrified to be a newborn in a hospital. More hours spent there means even more time to create damage and disease in newborns.

I will give you two answers to these problems. In

fact I will give you six solutions to these problems: home birth, home birth and home birth; breastfeeding, breastfeeding and breastfeeding! These are the two most awesome ways to circumvent so many pediatric problems.

It would be better for expectant parents to have no health insurance if it only forces them to deliver their babies in the hospital. It would be better for new parents to pay out of their pockets for a home birth than to be forced into the hospital. This would actually prove to be less expensive in the long run due to the superior long term health of infants born at home and breastfed from birth.

For these reasons I believe there are no such things as "Express Deliveries" of infants in hospitals and simultaneously there is no point to legislating a stay longer than this for infants and mothers. In and out in 24 hours really means in and out and in and out again and again — today, tomorrow, next week, next month, next year. The same unscientific, dangerous procedures as always are being performed. There is not enough time to recover from these procedure even if the mother and baby stay for a month in the hospital.

94% of all mothers should be delivering their babies in the safety of their own homes without hospital interventions and with far superior outcomes. I will admit that there are about 6 % of women who will benefit from hospital birth and that in these cases a healthier outcome will result with intervention. However, even the high risk cases in the hospital should go home as soon as the procedures are done to deliver the babies safely. The mothers should be with family, in constant communication with their doctors, with home health care services for the mother and baby, and in touch with lactation consultants or La Leche League leaders to make certain that the infants are 100% breastfed. Even these high risk cases should not be left alone in the hospitals to suffer from the abuses of the medical establishment."

Section Six

Additional Information

Information & Implementation

In keeping with the spirit of this book, it is essential we add information and implementation methods for the consumer. It is not enough to explain the dangers of hospital birth and the safety of home birth. I must help consumers take action on behalf of their families' emotional and physical well-being.

Implementation is what makes *The Home Birth Advantage* different from every other birthing book I have read. The reader can come away not only with information on home birth but with a safe birth plan to follow. The Homefirst® system is in place now for any healthy woman, regardless of age, to have a home birth.

One of the doctors on my staff recently said, "I like how consumers are getting smarter! Those consumers who have properly compared the home birth option with hospital offerings are the ones who return as our patients." He is absolutely right.

I would like to offer you some ways of becoming a wise consumer.

Therefore, I am listing specific contact names and numbers for those who wish to find out more about

Section Six: Additional Information

home birth and how to have a home birth.

About Homefirst Health Services

Homefirst Health Services is the largest physician practice specializing in home birth in the United States. Practicing in and around metropolitan Chicago, the staff of nearly 100 doctors, nurses and assistants is committed to the goal of providing every one of its patients with the safest and healthiest birth experience possible.

Most of Homefirst's patients are college educated, many in the fields of science and medicine themselves. They have carefully weighed modern birthing options and are coming to Homefirst to have their babies safely.

For some it is a lifestyle decision to reclaim control and responsibility for their own lives. Others are convinced of the safety and comfort of home birth, away from the noise and bright lights of the hospital. They all have in common the belief that a child conceived in love should be born in love. They have chosen the joy of natural childbirth through the guidance of doctors who are leaders in physician-attended home births.

Our Programs and Services for Consumers

All our programs and services are also listed on our web page. To access current Homefirst information contact us at http://www.homefirst.com or phone us at (847) 679-8336.

246

Speakers Bureau on Home Birth

If your childbirth class, women's group, professional or church organization is interested in any of the topics discussed in this book, please give us a call at
(847) 679-8336. The doctors of Homefirst Health Services are available to speak at your meetings.

Free Sunday Night Seminars on Home Birth

The newsletter also provides readers with a schedule of free Sunday night seminars given by the Homefirst staff. Seminars are open to anyone interested in finding out more about home birth and the philosophy and practice of Homefirst Health Services. The evening includes a video, a discussion with Homefirst Health Services medical staff, and a question and answer session.

The Homefirst Family Health Forum, Radio Program

Listeners are welcome to tune in or call in to "The Homefirst Family Health Forum", a one hour discussion and call-in radio program hosted by Dr. Mayer Eisenstein. For current radio station call letters and show times, check our web site at http://www.home-first.com or call (847) 679-8336. Topics discussed on the air include home birth, vaginal birth after cesarean section, breastfeeding, the impact on children of being at the birth of their siblings, vaccines and other current medical issues of interest to families, involved grandparents and friends. Our radio show newsletter, *Homefirst Family Health Forum*, which summarizes issues discussed on the air, may be subscribed to by calling (847) 679-8336. Subscription prices are also listed on our web site.

Home Birth Video Rental

Homefirst's own video, "The Home Court Advantage", is available at all office locations and through the mail. The film documents home birth through the experiences of families who have had babies at home with the Homefirst practice. Anyone wishing to know more about home birth through this medium may borrow a copy for home viewing. To receive a free rental copy through the mail, please send a $10.00 check for postage and handling to: Video, Homefirst Health Services, Administrative Office, 6400 N. Keating, Lincolnwood, Illinois 60712

Beatrice Tucker Fellowship Information

Any medical students, interns or residents who would like more information on how to apply for the Beatrice Tucker Fellowship may write to Dr. Mayer Eisenstein directly at Homefirst Health Services, Administrative Office, 6400 N. Keating, Lincolnwood, Illinois 60712.

Complimentary Conference With a Homefirst Physician

Homefirst offers free conferences by appointment to couples seeking more information about our services. Consultations are with one of the staff physicians and last approximately one hour. Couples are encouraged to inquire about home birth, nursing and home birth after cesarean section before making decisions about these very important matters. Call us at the above number for an appointment at our office nearest your home.

Homefirst Childbirth Classes

Preparing for a home birth is a unique experience. It is unlike preparing for a hospital delivery in many ways. Home birth parents need special information on preparing their homes, children, friends and families for birth and often have questions and concerns different from those covered in the more institutional childbirth classes. Being free of the influences of traditional hospital personnel, the classes cover the true meaning of natural delivery — delivery where drugs, IV fluids, episiotomies, electronic fetal monitors and other interventions are used routinely. For these reasons Homefirst offers its own childbirth preparation classes. Generally there are four home birth class sessions each two hours in length. They are taught by Homefirst's own nurses and held at the Homefirst offices in and around metropolitan Chicago. Anyone wishing more information on these classes may call us or visit our website.

Section Six: Additional Information

Second Opinions

It is the belief of Homefirst's staff that often families are given unscientific medical advice by their doctors on family health matters. Anyone who questions the opinion of his or her doctor should certainly seek a second opinion regarding breastfeeding, the use of technological interventions in pregnancy and birth, the safety of tests such as amniocentesis and ultrasound, the necessity of episiotomy, or repeat cesarean sections. Homefirst Health Services is pleased to offer second opinions to patients on these matters before decisions are made that they may later regret. To inquire about receiving a second opinion please call us at the above number.

Copies of The Home Birth Advantage Available

If you are unable to locate *The Home Birth Advantage* at your local library, please inform the librarian that library rate copies of the book are available by calling our administrative office in Lincolnwood. Copies are also available to the public through all Homefirst Health Services offices. To inquire about receiving a copy from our offices, please call (847) 679-8336 or visit our web site, www.homefirst.com.

Homefirst News

Our goal for this newsletter is to share vital information with our readers and to welcome you into the Homefirst family. Each issue will cover a different topic, i.e. immunization, home birth, breastfeeding, cancer treatment, mammography, etc. With the explosion of information on the Internet people now have the capability to research virtually any subject. In future issues we will help you explore the Internet as a resource and will give you addresses of important web sites. The Family Health Forum Newsletter will bring you scientific literature on critical issues in medicine. Most doctors will try to scare you about different diseases, Mayer Eisenstein will try to scare you about the treatment doctors will try to impose upon you.

The first two issues of the newsletter are complimentary and can be viewed on our website or by calling our administrative office at (847) 679-8336.

Part of our plan is to familiarize you with Homefirst Health Services. We encourage you to contact Homefirst to explore the possibility of having your baby at home, or having your family become a Homefirst family.

Dr. Eisenstein has integrated his 25 years in medicine, with his 30 years as a husband, father, and grandfather (six children and five grandchildren, the last ten born at home and all breastfed) to present a most entertaining and enlightening newsletter.

We are looking forward to hearing from you and to sharing the latest scientific findings. Our aim is to help our families enjoy to the fullest the precious gift of life that G-d gave us.

Homefirst Newsletters

The following is a listing of topics covered in the *Homefirst News.*

A complimentary issue, a back issue or a subscription to Homefirst News is available by calling

(847) 679-8336 or by consulting our web site for further details at www.homefirst.com

Vol. I No. 1
Ear Infections and Antibiotics
If your child develops an ear infection should you treat with antibiotics??? The answer in the past was 100% yes! However, there is mounting scientific evidence that not only are antibiotics the wrong treatment, but it can lead to problems such as recurrent ear infections, hearing loss, as well as total body resistance to more serious types of infections.

Vol. I No. 2
The Birth Control "Pill" — Unavoidably Dangerous
No other drug in the Physician's Desk Reference has

as long a description of side effects as the birth control "PILL". Breast cancer, cardiovascular disease, blood clots, liver tumors, high blood pressure, infertility, sterility, and abortion are some of the more serious problems associated with the "PILL". In fact, the new third generation "PILL" seems to be more dangerous than the previous ones.

Vol. I No. 3
Chicken Pox Vaccine and Hep. B Vaccine — Raising Ethical and Moral Dilemmas
I have chosen to discuss the Varivax Vaccine (Chicken Pox Vaccine) and the Hepatitis B Vaccine. These two vaccines raise ethical and moral dilemmas, as well as issues of safety. The Chicken Pox Vaccine is grown on the tissue of aborted human babies and the Hepatitis B Vaccine is meant to protect against Hepatitis B, a blood borne and sexually transmitted disease. I want to raise doubt in your mind as to the safety, efficacy and moral issues of vaccines.

Vol. I No. 4
Infant "Formula" — A "recipe" of cow's milk, sugar & water...
Eat at Mom's
Artificial feeding is an attempt to fool nature but the bottom line is that it can't happen. Our society is paying heavily with the health and very lives of our children by providing an inferior imitation of nature's nutritional plan. Breast milk is a precious natural resource that we, in our society, are all too willing to waste. It is every bit

254

as essential to our children's growth as adequate rainfall is to the growth of our farmers' crops.

Vol. I   No. 5
Electronic Fetal Monitoring or Electronic Feeble
Monitoring
The outstanding individual scientific works from
1973 through 1996 by Drs. Haverkamp, Hon,
Landendoerfer, Shy, Nelson, Thacker and Luthy have
quite conclusively shown that electronic fetal monitoring
is not superior to auscultation. Read the full articles for
more detailed information about the worthlessness of
electronic fetal monitoring. Please check the list of refer-
ences.

Vol. I   No. 6
Asthma & Allergy —- Caused by Bottle Feeding,
Hospital Birth and Vaccinations???
The overall goal is to minimize medical care and
maximize time honored remedies. Of most importance
we can reduce the incidence of asthma and allergy by
nursing our children, influencing our grandchildren to
nurse and by staying away from dangerous drugs & vaccines.

Vol. I   No. 7
Mammograms or Mammoscams??
Mammography, long hailed as the most effective
screening "prevention" method for breast cancer, is over-
rated. Its risks to pre-menopausal women especially -
false alarms, missed cancers, spread of early undiag-

nosed cancer caused by breast compression, and radiation to the breast-far outweigh its negligible benefits.

Vol. I No. 8
Emerging Viruses — Are Vaccines Contaminated?? - Part I
The FDA is reluctant to admit its lack of knowledge about vaccines to the medical/scientific community. Yet, practicing physicians are expected to unquestionably endorse the safety of vaccines under all circumstances and to all individuals.

Vol. II No. 1
Emerging Viruses - Are Vaccines Contaminated?? - Part II
There are multiple viral contaminants to American made vaccines. Dr. W. John Martin, Professor of Pathology at the University of Southern California, noted that the increased incidence of chronic fatigue syndrome, attention deficit hyperactivity disorder, autism, and other behavior linked illnesses "may be an inadvertent consequence of stealth virus vaccine contaminants."

Vol. II No. 2
Why Home Birth?
"There is no convincing or compelling evidence that hospitals give a better guarantee of the safety of the majority of mother and babies. It is possible that the contrary may be the case."

Vol. II   No. 3

Home Birth After Cesarean — Exposing the Cesarean Myth

The maternal mortality from c-section is 10 to 20 times greater than from a vaginal delivery. Despite all of the scientific evidence, since the 1980s, showing that the c-section rate is too high [25-30% in United States hospitals as opposed to less than 5% by home birth physicians], the rate continues to climb. The countries which continue to have the lowest c-section rates, (i.e. Norway, Denmark, Sweden, Holland, Japan, etc.) continue to have the lowest infant and maternal mortality rates in the world.

Vol. II   No. 4

The Pill an Abortifacient

In addition to all the serious side effects of the Pill (i.e. blood clots, stroke, high blood pressure, breast cancer, etc. to name just a few), the Pill causes abortions.

Vol. II   No. 5

The Flu Vaccine an Unnecessary Risk

At the present time, your doctor will try to scare you about the flu, until all the evidence is in, Mayer Eisenstein, M.D., will scare you about the flu vaccine. My advice is "Say No" to the flu vaccine. If you get the flu ask your grandmother for her chicken soup recipe since one grandmother is still worth at least two physicians!

Section Six: Additional Information

Vol. II   No. 6

Ritalin — The Drugging of our School Chidren

Scientific studies have documented: the sudden death caused by Ritalin; the abnormal brain functions caused by Ritalin; the growth suppression caused by Ritalin; the neurological tics caused by Ritalin; agitation, addiction and psychosis caused by Ritalin. How many more of our children will have to be exposed to dangerous drugs such as Ritalin prescribed by our pediatricians and psychiatrists before we "wake up"?

Vol. III   No. 1

Just Say No — Heb B Vaccine

In this issue we will also bring you some of the preliminary work of Dr. Bonnie Dunbar, Professor of Cell Biology at Baylor College of Medicine. Dr. Dunbar has been compiling data on the association between hepatitis B vaccine and Chronic Fatigue Syndrome (CFS), Multiple Sclerosis (MS) and various other auto-immune diseases. ...Until we get a full disclosure of the risks vs. the benefits it would be foolish to continue a program of mass vaccination.

Vol. III   No. 2

Complimentary Issue — Natural Progesterone Cream

The following symptoms have been associated with Estrogen Overload Syndrome:

PMS; fibrocystic breast disease; endometriosis; menopausal symptoms; fibroids; ...

About 50 years ago scientists discovered that the

258

Mexican wild yam contains substances which are chemically similar to human progesterone. This natural Mexican wild yam product can act just like the body's own natural progesterone and relieve many of the above symptoms.

Vol. III   No. 3

Complimentary Issue — Benign Prostatic Hypertrophy

Somewhere between the ages of 30 and 40 a man's prostate begins to enlarge. BPH will affect nearly all men as they age. What is generally not known is the fact that there are safe, natural and effective ways of dealing with BPH. By age 50 more than 50% of men will have prostate surgery, radiation treatment, or will be on prescription drugs like Proscar (finasteride). Finasteride has been shown to cause impotence (in more than 60% of patients1), decreased libido, decreased amount of semen per ejaculation, breast tenderness, breast enlargement, lip swelling and skin rashes.

Vol. III   No. 4

Low Carbohydrate Lifestyle

"Dieting may be the major cause of obesity" — Jean-Paul Deslypere, University of Ghent Professor of Human Nutrition

High carbohydrate, low fat diets for weight loss, are the current medical recommendations. In the last decade Americans have reduced their fat intake, only to get fatter than ever. For the first time in history, a

Section Six: Additional Information

majority of males are overweight. The previously reported relationship between higher fat consumption and
resulting obesity has not been proven by scientific studies. Previously reported associations between higher fat
consumption and breast cancer have been refuted. A
14-year study of nearly 89,000 women found no evidence that a high-fat diet promotes breast cancer or
that a low-fat diet protects against it. Women who ate
the least fat appeared to have a 15 percent higher rate
of breast cancer. (Journal of the American Medical
Association 3/10/99) The low fat/low cholesterol diet is
ineffective. Some scientists now think that the low-
fat/high carbohydrate diets are actually making us fat.

Vol. III   No. 5
The Pill & Hormone Replacement Therapy —
Unavoidably Dangerous

Did G-d make American women deficient in estrogen and progesterone? Does every American woman
need synthetic chemical estrogen or progesterone chem-
icals when they reach menopause? Do synthetic hor-
mones protect you from heart disease and osteoporosis?
Is a synthetic hormone, which is structurally different,
better than the actual natural hormone? Is every phase
of our lives a condition that must be treated with chemical drugs?

Vol. III   No. 6
Estrogen the Common Link to Breast Cancer
"The evidence is overwhelming that estrogen is inti-

260

mately connected to the development of most breast cancers. Estrogen encourages breast cells to divide more often and more rapidly. Thus, if a mutation (inherited or triggered by a carcinogen) lies imbedded in the DNA, cancer cells are more likely to proliferate when high estrogen levels are present. (The main reason men, who also have breast and breast tissue rarely develop breast cancer is that their exposure to estrogen is minimal.) This also may help to explain why breast cancer rates have increased in tandem with the widespread use of birth control pills and estrogen replacement therapy, both of which increase the amount of estrogen circulating in a woman's body over her lifetime.

 *Further Reading*

Newsletters, Periodicals

Benaron, Harry B., M.D. & Tucker, Beatrice E., M.D., "Maternal Mortality of the Chicago Maternity Center," *American Journal of Public Health*, Volume 27, January 1937.

"C-Section Experience of Northern Illinois, Inc.", brochure of the support group for cesarean parents, 1220 Gentry Road, Hoffman Estates, IL 60195

"Chicago's Dr. Joseph B. DeLee," *Time* Magazine, Volume XXVII Number 21, May 25, 1936

Hooker, Ransom S., M.D., F.A.C.S., "Maternal Mortality in New York City, a study of all puerperal deaths 1930-1933," Oxford University Press, 1933

Jelliffe, D. B.,& Jelliffe, E.F.P., "The Uniqueness of Human Milk," *Am. J. Clinical Nutrition*, 24 (Aug. 1971).

Section Six: Additional Information

La Leche League News, 1400 N. Meacham Rd. Schaumburg, Ill. 60173 (847) 519-7730

Manley, Marc, M.D., M.P.H.; Tanio, Craig, B.A.; & Wolfe, Sidney M., M.D. "Unnecessary Cesarean Sections, A Rapidly Growing National Epidemic," Public Citizen Health Research Group, Washington, D.C., 1986

NAPSAC NEWS, publication of The International Association of Parents and Professionals for Safe Alternatives in Childbirth, P.O. Box 428, Marble Hill, Mo. 63764

Ratner, Herbert, M.D., "The Natural Institution of the Family
(Marriage: An office of Nature)," 1987, an address delivered at the tenth convention of the Fellowship of Catholic Scholars

Ratner, Herbert, M.D., editor, *Child and Family Magazine*, a quarterly survey on the family, 244 S. Wesley, Oak Park, Il 60302

Sessions Rugh, Susan, "Being Born in Chicago," Chicago History, *The Magazine of the Chicago Historical Society*, Volume XV, Number 4, Winter 1986-87

Tews, Marjorie, "Do Obstetrical Intranatal Interventions Make Birth Safer?," *British Journal of Obstetrics and Gynecology*, July, 1986

The People's Doctor, A Medical Newsletter for Consumers, P.O. Box 982, Evanston, IL 60204

Books

Cohen, Nancy Wainer, & Estner, Lois J., *Silent Knife, Cesarean Prevention and Vaginal Birth After Cesarean*, (Massachusetts, Bergin and Garvey, 1983)

Hathaway, Marjie, & Jay Hathaway, *Children at Birth*, (Sherman Oaks, Ca,: Academy, 1978)

Leavitt, Judith Walzer, *Brought to Bed, Childbearing in America* 1750-1950,
(Oxford University Press, 1986)

Mendelsohn, Robert, M.D., *Confessions of a Medical Heretic*, (Chicago, Contemporary Books, Inc., 1979)

Mendelsohn, Robert, M.D., *Mal(e) Practice*, (Chicago, Contemporary Books, Inc., 1981)

Oakley, Ann, *The Captured Womb, A History of the Medical Care of Pregnant Women*, (New York, Basil Blackwell Publishers, Inc., 1984)

Semmelweis, Ignaz, *The Etiology, Concept, and Prophylaxis of Childbed Fever*, translated by K. Codell Carter, (Madison, University of Wisconsin Press, Ltd., 1983)

Section Six: Additional Information

Stewart, David, & Stewart, Lee, *Safe Alternatives in Childbirth* (Chapel Hill, N.C.: NAPSAC, 1976)

Stewart, David, & Stewart, Lee, 21st Century *Obstetrics NOW!* (Marble Hill, Mo.: NAPSAC, 1977)

The Womanly Art of Breastfeeding, 1400 N. Meacham Rd. Schaumburg, Ill. 60173 (847) 519-7730, 1981)

Thompson, Morton, *The Cry and the Covenant*, (London, Heinemann, 1951)

Wertz, Richard W., and Wertz, Dorothy C., *Lying In*, (New York, The Free Press, a division of Macmillan, 1977)

Index

Pregnancy Journal

Oh that my words were written down!
Oh that they were printed in a book!
— Job 19:23

The first month of pregnancy
The baby's spinal column and brain are
beginning to develop.
Length 1/8"

The second month of pregnancy

The baby's internal and genital organs are formed. The baby's heart is already beating. Length 1"

The third month of pregnancy

The baby's toes and fingers are fully formed.
The baby is moving around, even though you cannot feel it.
Length 3", weight 1 oz.

Pregnancy Journal

The fourth month of pregnancy

The baby is fully formed. Eyebrows and lashes are growing.

Length 6', weight 5 oz.

The fifth month of pregnancy
The teeth are forming in the jaw and hair on the head.

Length 10", weight 1 lb.

The sixth month of pregnancy

The baby is growing and can suck its thumb.
Length 13", weight 2 lbs.

Section Six: Additional Information

The seventh month of pregnancy
The lungs are beginning to mature. The vernix is covering the skin for protection.
Length 14", weight 2.5 lbs.

Pregnancy Journal

The eighth month of pregnancy
Strong and vigorous movements are clearly felt.
Length 16", weight 4 lbs.

Pregnancy Journal

The ninth month of pregnancy

The baby grows approximately one to two ounces a day. The iris of the eye is blue.
Length 18", weight 6 lbs.

Pregnancy Journal

About the Author

He is on the Professional Board of the Family Life League, Council for the Jewish Elderly, Task Force Council on Education for Public Health — Medical College of Wisconsin, and on the Editorial Board for *Child and Family Magazine*. He is the author of the award winning book *Give Birth at Home With The Home Court Advantage*, as well as the editor for the "Family Health Forum" newsletter. His medical film "Primum Non Nocere" (Above All Do No Harm), a documentary on home birth, was an award winner at the Chicago Film Festival in 1987.

Some of his guest appearances include: the "Phil Donahue Show", "Milt Rosenberg Show", "Today in Chicago", "Ask the Expert", "Daybreak", "Oprah Winfrey Show", "Ed Schwartz Radio Show". "WMAQ TV news 'Unnecessary Hysterectomy'", "Chicago Fox TV News - 'Immunizations — Are They Necessary'", CBC Newsworld Canada - "Are Mass Immunizations Necessary".

Since 1987, his weekly radio show "Family Health Forum", has aired in the Chicagoland area. In September 1998 "Family Health Forum" became nationally syndicated. In the live call-in format, all listener's comments, questions or medical experiences are welcome by Dr. Eisenstein.

Dr. Eisenstein's philosophy comes from his years in medicine, combined with his years as a husband, father, and grandfather (he has six children and five grandchildren).

About the Author

Dr. Mayer Eisenstein is a graduate of the University of Illinois Medical School, the Medical College of Wisconsin School of Public Health, and the John Marshall Law School.

Since 1973 he has been in private medical practice and is currently the Medical Director of Homefirst® Health Services, the largest physician attended home birth service in the country. In his 26 years in medicine, he and his practice have delivered over 14,000 babies at home, as well as cared for over 60,000 parents, grandparents and children. Now, Dr. Eisenstein and his practice are delivering second generation babies for women who themselves were born at home with his practice.

He is Board Certified by the National Board of Medical Examiners, American Board of Public Health and Preventive Medicine, and the American Board of Quality Assurance and Utilization Review Physicians. He is a member of the National Honor Society. He is a recipient of the Howard Fellowship, Health Professional Scholarship, University of Illinois School of Medicine Scholarship, and is a member of the Dean's List at John Marshall Law School.

290